RECREATION MANAGEMENT AND PRICING

Cover illustration courtesy of Staffordshire County Council, Shugborough Estate.

Recreation Management and Pricing

The Effect of Charging Policy on Demand at Countryside Recreation Sites

A. G. BOVAIRD
University of Aston at Birmingham

M. J. TRICKER
University of Aston at Birmingham

R. STOAKES
London Borough of Greenwich

Gower

Published by
Gower Publishing Company Limited,
Gower House, Croft Road, Aldershot, Hampshire GU11 3HR, England

and

Gower Publishing Company,
Old Post Road, Brookfield, Vermont 05036, U.S.A.

British Library Cataloguing in Publication Data

Bovaird, Tony
Recreation management and pricing.
1. Recreation areas---Great Britain---Utilization
2. Recreation areas---Great Britain---Admission charges
I. Title II. Tricker, Mike III. Stoakes, Robbie
338.78'17 GV75

Library of Congress Cataloging in Publication Data

Bovaird, Tony, 1949-
Recreation management and pricing.

Bibliography: p.
1. Recreation areas--Great Britain--Management.
2. Recreation areas--Great Britain--Finance. 3. Recreation areas--Great Britain--Visitors. 4. Recreational surveys--Great Britain. I. Tricker, Mike, 1949-
II. Stoakes, Robbie, 1948- . III. Title.
GV182.15.B68 1984 790'.0941 84-10151
ISBN 0-566-00671-5

Printed in Great Britain by Biddles Ltd, Guildford, Surrey

Contents

Figures

Tables

Preface

This book derives from a research study of the influence of pricing policies on visitor use of countryside recreation facilities undertaken by the authors between September 1980 and November 1982. This study was sponsored by the Countryside Commission as part of their research programme on recreation management and policy. We would like to acknowledge the debt of gratitude we owe to the Commission's staff for the cooperation and positive assistance which they provided at all stages of the research. Particular thanks are due to Roger Sidaway and David Champion for their help in setting up the project and monitoring its progress. Without their support and the vision of the Commission, this highly ambitious project could not have been completed.

We would also like to express our gratitude to the numerous members of the staff of the National Trust and the Department of Environment whose cooperation enabled us to assemble an extensive data base which is perhaps uniquely suited to an analysis of recreation demand. We are particularly grateful to Michael Beaumont of the National Trust, John Hobson and Brian Bayliss of the Department of the Environment for their advice and guidance in the interpretation of this data and for the insights which they provided on the development of pricing policies. In addition to providing access to disaggregated data, the regional administrators of the National Trust, and the managers of the sites selected for detailed study were kind enough to discuss the results of the statistical analysis and to provide detailed advice on the local factors which aided their interpretation. Lois Bowser and Paul Jeffrey also provided valuable assistance in the early stages of the research.

During the various stages of this study and the preparation of this book, one of the authors' greatest consolations was the knowledge that it was at least as difficult to type as it was to write. Our grateful thanks must therefore go to Kas Davies, Cheryl Edkins, Tracey Elson, Jenny Hipkiss and Jean Roche for the skill, patience and forbearance which they displayed. Responsibility for any errors and omissions, however, remains ours alone.

Tony Bovaird,
Mike Tricker,
Public Sector Management Group,
University of Aston

Robbie Stoakes,
Assistant Director,
Leisure Services,
Greenwich
(formerly Economist at the
Countryside Commission)

1 The role of pricing in the management of countryside recreational facilities

Scope and purpose of the study

As a result of the financial stringency which has prevailed in recent years, increasing interest has been shown by local authorities and grant aiding bodies in alternative means of financing countryside recreation facilities. There has also been a growing awareness on the part of recreation managers of the potential for adopting improved marketing approaches, in which pricing policy plays a part. The scope for change has been highlighted in, for example, the Rufford Country Park Marketing Study (Countryside Commission 1979) and the Cragside Marketing Study (Countryside Commission 1981).

If countryside recreation managers are to be able to raise revenue and to regulate demand, it is clearly essential to know the resistance of visitors to different levels of charges. Despite the large body of literature dealing with recreational demand from a theoretical standpoint and the increasing volume of research into the market for leisure activities in general, there is a surprising lack of knowledge about the effects of alternative pricing strategies on visitor use of facilities. Thus, whilst the principles and potential of pricing policies for countryside recreation facilities have been comprehensively reviewed (Stoakes 1976; McCallum 1979), very few systematic empirical investigations of the effects of price changes on demand have been undertaken (Snaith 1975; CRRAG 1977). Consequently, little guidance is available to site owners and managers on the actual relationship between levels of charges and levels of use or on the most appropriate pricing strategy to adopt in order to meet local needs and circumstances.

Given the need for operational guidelines which can be adopted quickly and adapted by local managers, rigorous models of demand for individual recreational facilities are not the immediate concern. Rather, relatively simple statistical analysis of the past use of recreation facilities under various types of pricing structure and management, together with in-depth case studies of the impact of particular pricing and marketing policies are likely to produce the most useful results. This study, therefore, concentrates on the areas of pricing policy where little guidance is currently available to site operators. The book has four main objectives:

(i) To examine and analyse existing evidence on the price - visitor relationship.

(ii) To seek to identify the factors which influence the relationship between admission prices and visits to country parks and equivalent sites.

(iii) To establish an operational framework for data analysis and presentation which will allow operators, and grant aiding bodies, such as the Countryside Commission, to achieve more systematic monitoring and evaluation of pricing policies adopted by local authorities and other operators.

(iv) To validate the results of statistical analysis by in-depth examination of specific case studies.

The Countryside Commission, in the project brief which initiated this research, laid special emphasis on the need to learn more about the effects of different pricing policies on admissions to country parks. However, the data available for statistical analysis of admissions to country parks was insufficient to generate reliable results. This study therefore, has concentrated on research into patterns of use at National Trust properties and Department of the Environment (DoE) historic buildings and ancient monuments located in rural areas, which were felt to be analogous sites in terms of their attraction of countryside visitors. Particular attention has been given to those National Trust and DoE properties with large areas of open land available for informal recreation, and which are therefore most similar to local authority country parks.

Why is pricing important?

There are three main reasons why pricing is important in the management of countryside recreation facilities. These relate to three fundamental aspects of recreation planning and management - obtaining information on visitor preferences, raising revenue and regulating demand.

(i) Obtaining information on visitor preferences

By monitoring reactions to variations in admission prices, site managers can generate information about visitors' valuation of the facilities provided - their 'revealed preferences'. If visitors are willing to pay less for some sites than for others, or less for countryside sites in general than for other recreational facilities, then we get an insight into the relative values they place on these facilities. The alternative approach of using visitor numbers alone can be misleading. Thus, there is a danger that a site with low visitor numbers may be regarded as a failure, whereas the intensity of enjoyment of those visitors may be very high. Conversely, sites with high visitor numbers may not be especially successful, both because of the damage done to the amenity of the site and because, for many visitors, other sites might well provide very adequate substitutes. Analysing the relationship between variations in admission prices and variations in usage can help to identify the intensity of visitor preferences. For individual sites this allows site managers to identify those types of facilities which are likely to be more cost-effective. For funding agencies such information may help in deciding how funds should be allocated. Of course, monitoring the relationship between the level and structure of charges and patterns of visitor behaviour is only one of the ways open to management for eliciting information on the needs/preferences of visitors, but the potential value of this method has often been sadly neglected in the past.

(ii) Revenue raising

The period since 1974 has seen the need for site managers to raise revenue become increasingly important as public sector agencies have found their budgets frozen or cut in real terms. Managers have also seen revenue obtained from visitors as a means of financing the development of individual sites (or other sites), promoting their attractions, or protecting them from the effects of budget cuts.

(iii) Demand regulation

Pricing can also be used to restrict demand to the supply available. Where demand or supply varies over time, different levels of charges can be set in order to ensure, for example, that demand and supply are balanced. This is a fundamental principle of resource allocation but one which can bring political and administrative difficulties. Many countryside recreation facilities become overcrowded at certain times of the year. This increases the operators' costs, decreases the satisfaction of users at these times and can result in excessive damage to some sites. Adopting a pricing system which deters some of the peak demand can therefore help to decrease costs, increase satisfaction of users and protect the amenity of a site. Varying prices between peak and off-peak periods can also operate to defer the need for investment related to peak capacity. This situation is not, of course, peculiar to countryside recreation facilities. It is a common practice in energy supply and transport, notably among electricity undertakings and railways.

The relative importance of these three aspects of pricing policy will vary, depending not only upon the local constraints on demand and operating capacity at individual sites, but also upon the political and economic climate within which the provision of facilities takes place. While all three aspects of pricing policy are potentially important in site management, it must be acknowledged that in certain circumstances charging may not be appropriate, so that financing must be carried out by voluntary subscription or through general taxation. This book is not, therefore, concerned with providing a case for the introduction of charges at all countryside recreation sites; instead it aims to explore the possible implications of the use of charges as a means of achieving the overall objectives of recreation provision.

What is the relationship between admission prices and visitor use?

In order to predict the effects of changes in admission prices on revenue it is important to know the relationship between changes in prices and visitor numbers. It is also the knowledge of this relationship which gives the most direct information on visitor preferences. The most usual way of presenting this relationship is in the form of a market demand curve, as in Figure 1.1 . In general, it is expected that for most goods or services an increase in price will result in a decrease in the quantity consumed.

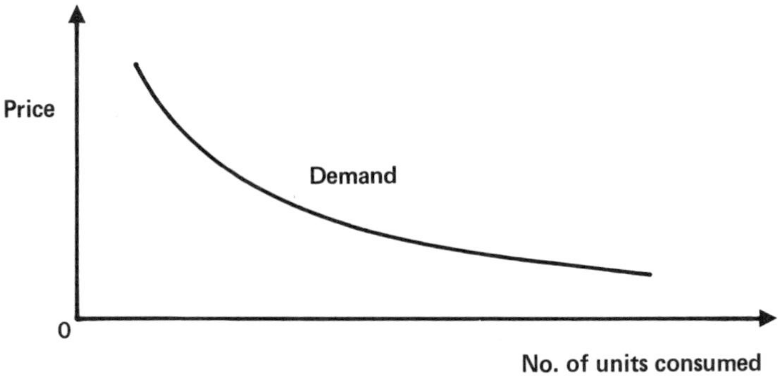

Figure 1.1 **Typical Form of a Demand Curve**

In such a market, suppliers can be categorised as either 'price takers' (when they have to accept the going 'market price' if they wish to make significant sales), or 'price setters' (when they face an imperfectly competitive market, so that they can raise prices without necessarily losing much of their demand). Suppliers who can act as price setters are obviously in a more powerful market position. In most circumstances, however, suppliers must take care in determining the precise level at which to set prices since too high a price might seriously deter demand and possibly reduce sales revenue. Therefore, suppliers must estimate the degree of responsiveness of demand to price changes. This responsiveness is measured by the price elasticity of demand which is defined as the ratio of the percentage change in the quantity consumed to the percentage change in the price.

Three possible cases which might apply in specific circumstances are illustrated in Figure 1.2. In situation (a), the demand curve is of such a shape that a 1% increase in price results in a 1% decrease in consumption. This is known as unitary price elasticity of demand (i.e. price elasticity of demand equals -1). It can be seen from the figure that as price increases from P_1 to P_2, demand falls from Q_1 to Q_2 and revenue changes from $OP_1 \times Q_1$ to $OP_2 \times Q_2$. In the case of unitary elasticity, total revenue is in fact identical at all prices, since price changes are exactly offset by equal and opposite changes in the quantity consumed.

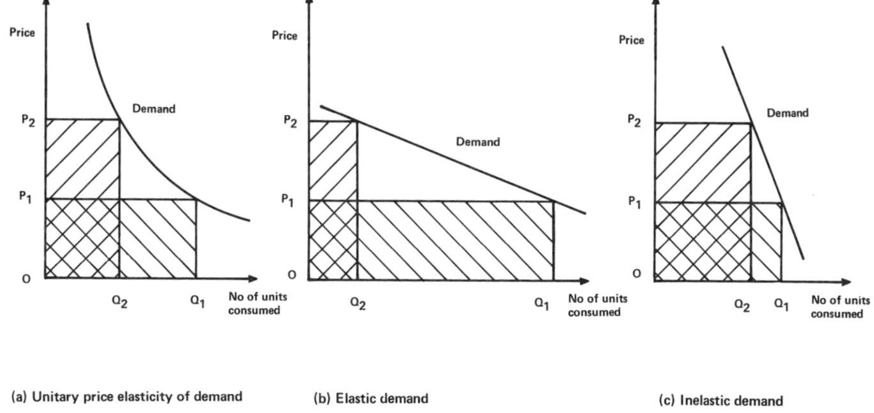

(a) Unitary price elasticity of demand   (b) Elastic demand   (c) Inelastic demand

Figure 1.2   Price elasticity of demand

In situation (b), demand decreases more than proportionately when price rises from P to P . This is a case of elastic demand (i.e. price elasticity of demand lies in the range from -1 to - infinity). In this case, revenue falls as price increases.

In situation (c), demand decreases less than proportionately when price rises from P to P . This is a case of inelastic demand (i.e. price elasticity of demand lies in the range of 0 to -1). With such a demand curve, revenue increases as price rises.

Goods and services which exhibit an inelastic demand in a particular market offer two opportunities for their suppliers to increase their profits. Firstly, if price is increased, total revenue will increase. Secondly, if some demand is deterred by this price rise, then the operating costs may also fall. It is therefore generally to be expected that private sector suppliers of goods and services will attempt to increase prices to levels at which demand becomes price elastic, i.e. in the range -1 to - infinity.

Is countryside recreation demand different?

Is there any reason to suppose that countryside recreation facilities are different from other goods and services for which demand analysis has been carried out? The three key elements to consider are the nature of the 'product', the nature of the suppliers and the nature of the demand.

(i) The nature of the 'product'

Countryside recreation facilities offer such a wide variety of recreational experiences at such a wide range of prices that no single market can be said to exist. Yet visits to all the countryside facilities included in the present study appear to reflect similar trends, and differences between them seem likely to be more a matter of degree than of kind. Recreation sites, though they exist as physical entities and are, indeed, often man-made, can be regarded as a service: they provide a recreational experience or series of experiences which cannot be tested or sampled in advance. The major 'product' is the experience of the visit. Recreation sites therefore compete with each other in terms of being able to provide a valued recreational experience.

(ii) The nature of the suppliers

The individuals and organisations responsible for providing and managing countryside recreation facilities may be regarded as <u>price setters.</u> Thus, although they may experience competion from other similar facilities in their neighbourhood, they can increase their prices without complete loss of sales. This implies that they either have 'market power' (i.e. they have erected and can maintain effective barriers to the competitive activity of other actual or potential local suppliers) or else they have significant 'customer loyalty' (perhaps because of the special qualities of a site, or because of effective marketing). However, all sites included in the present study were at least partly constrained in their pricing and marketing policy by the existence of competitors.

(iii) The nature of the demand

Potential visitors to countryside recreational facilities are dispersed, so that time and money spent on travel are likely to be important in addition to any charge paid to gain admission to a facility. This is by no means a unique factor since it also applies, for example, to major retail outlets in city centres or out-of-town locations.

Perhaps the most important feature of demand for countryside recreation is, however, that visitors do not just visit particular sites; they undertake a recreational experience on each trip of which the visit to the site is only a part. The demand for this recreational trip and demand for the particular site visit will be influenced by different factors; and admission prices are likely to affect these demand functions in different ways.

Other factors which may affect demand cause complications and, in order to isolate the influence of admission prices, we need to take account of the effect of these on visitors. To do this, it is necessary to know what the most important influences are; what effects they have; and how they change over time. In this book the influences of weather, incomes, petrol costs, site promotion and special events are analysed, where possible, together with a range of other variables. This is not a straightforward exercise and it has not often been attempted in the past. This has meant that previous judgements about the effects of admission prices have been greatly misleading, since they have not isolated the influence of many other factors from that of price changes. Despite the difficulties outlined here, the analysis described in this book leads us to the conclusion that demand analysis is as useful for countryside recreation facilities as for other goods and services and can provide estimates of price elasticity for facilities which are sufficiently reliable to be useful for planning and management purposes.

Wider implications of pricing policy

The fact that this study seeks to establish the relationship between pricing policies and patterns of visits to countryside recreation facilities does not mean that the authors consider that pricing will be appropriate in all circumstances. Indeed, pricing may sometimes be technically or economically inefficient and there may be overriding social considerations in some cases.

Technically, the use of pricing may be inefficient in situations where the exclusion of visitors (for example, by fencing off properties) would be impractical or much too expensive. With low visitor numbers, the costs of collection of admission charges may also sometimes outweigh the income. In addition, pricing may not be economically efficient if it causes harmful side-effects (such as damage to the rest of the countryside because of diversion of recreation activity to non-priced facilities) or brings about the under-utilisation of facilities and amenities which have a very low marginal cost of provision. To test the validity of these objections to pricing, information on the extent of these side-effects and the relationship of marginal costs to prices is needed. To date, very little information of this kind has been systematically collected.

It has also been argued that charging for countryside recreation facilities is regressive; that is, it discriminates against low income households. While the equity effects of recreation provision are clearly important, it does not seem sensible to make general judgements on the equity effects of pricing without considering the detailed circumstances of individual sites. Although there is some evidence that usage of countryside recreation sites is biased towards high and middle-income households, and especially towards car-owning households (Fitton 1979), no general presumption should be made about the equity effects of introducing or increasing charges. The present study should not, therefore, be seen as an attempt to advocate the introduction of admission charges at all countryside recreation sites. Rather it is concerned with the possible implications of such charges as a means of achieving the overall purposes of recreation provision.

Structure of the book

In Chapter 2, the pricing policies of local authorities, the Department of the Environment, the National Trust and private operators are examined. Chapter 3 reviews recent trends in recreational visits at the national level. Chapter 4 considers the special characteristics of demand for countryside recreation in more detail. Chapter 5 explains the variety of statistical approaches adopted to identify the effects of variations in admission prices on visits to countryside recreation facilities. Chapters 6 and 7 give the results of the statistical analysis of the influence of admission prices and other factors upon demand at Department of Environment and National Trust sites. Chapters 8 and 9 present the results of a more detailed analysis of the factors influencing demand at a number of individual sites. Chapter 10 contains a discussion on the alternative pricing options open to site managers and their effects on patterns of visits. Chapter 11 summarises the results of the analysis and puts forward a series of recommendations on the basis of these findings.

2 Pricing policies for countryside recreational facilities

Introduction

In this chapter, we discuss the choices which are open to site operators in designing pricing structures for their facilities. An outline is then given of the policies adopted by the Department of Environment, the National Trust, local authorities and private operators with respect to the level and structure of their prices in the period since 1968.

Options for pricing structure

A site operator has to design a charging structure which reflects optimum decisions on where, when, upon whom and how to levy charges.

Where to charge involves choices between charges at entrances, car parks, separate facilities within the site, or some combination of these.

When to charge involves choices between charges all the year round at the same rate, or differentially in each season and/or on Sundays and Bank Holidays, or differentially on certain peak days only.

Whom to charge involves decisions on concessionary rates to certain categories of visitor - most typically children, pensioners, coach parties booked in advance but increasingly also to the unemployed.

How to charge involves choices between different technical systems of collecting charges. It also involves decisions on whether or not to set up a membership (or season ticket) scheme and the classes of membership within such a scheme. In addition, some operators may need to decide whether or not to join with neighbouring sites in offering joint tickets at concessionary rates.

Clearly there are many permutations open to operators in combining these different elements of pricing structure. No single pricing structure seems likely to be suitable to the circumstances of all, or even a majority of sites. The following sections consider the approaches which have been taken by different operators on the levels and structures of admission prices. Later chapters examine available evidence on the effects of some of these pricing structures on patterns of visitor use and the circumstances in which they are likely to be appropriate.

Pricing policies of the main operators

The Department of the Environment

Given their limited range of facilities, ancient monuments and historic buildings in the care of the Department of the Environment generally do not lend themselves to separate charges for car parks or individual facilities, so they normally have a single all-in admission price. Discounts on the full adult admission price are available for children, old age pensioners and for parties of 12 or more. Season ticket holders and parties of school children undertaking educational visits are allowed in free of charge. In some instances, where properties are open throughout the year, and particularly in recognised holiday centres, slightly lower levels of charges are operated during the period from October to March. The schedule of charges is normally prominently displayed at the site entrance as well as at the ticket office.

Until the 1960's the DoE's pricing policy was very simple, consisting of one price for the major monuments and another (lower) rate for the minor ones. Subsequently, some attempt was made to differentiate prices according to the attractiveness of properties, the facilities available, and the time of year. At a few of the very popular monuments, prices have been increased at an above average rate in recent years to prevent overcrowding (Holman 1979).

In general, charges for admission were maintained at a relatively low money price in the early years of the period studied and the range of prices at any one time was relatively narrow. Thus, until 1976, the charge for the vast majority of sites was less than 10 pence and for more than half was 5 pence or less (Table 2.1).

Table 2.1

Distribution of adult admission prices (pence) at DoE sites in England

Years	1-5	6-10	11-20	21-30	31-40	41-50	51-75	76-100	101+	NA
1968										123
1969										123
1970	91	22	5	-	-	-	-	-	-	5
1971	92	22	5	-	-	-	-	-	-	4
1972	94	22	5	-	-	-	-	-	-	2
1973	78	28	11	1	1	-	-	-	-	2
1974	79	28	11	3	1	-	-	-	-	1
1975	78	28	11	3	1	-	-	-	-	2
1976	-	70	35	8	5	4	-	1	-	1
1977	-	69	35	8	4	4	-	1	-	2
1978	-	3	80	2	6	3	3	1	1	13
1979	-	3	79	16	6	3	3	1	1	11
1980	-	-	-	88	17	-	8	3	2	5

Reviews of the level of charges which have taken place at intervals of two or three years have resulted in increases which, although modest in absolute terms, have been substantial when viewed in percentage terms - averaging 28% in 1973; 103% in 1976; 41% in 1978 and 59% in 1980. Whilst in many instances these periodic increases did little more than restore real prices to their 1970 levels, in the case of some sites, they resulted in more than a doubling of real prices over the period studied. In the periods between price rises inflation resulted in a substantial erosion of real prices.

Some examples of price changes at particular DoE sites are given in Table 2.2. This table indicates that the 300% price rise at a site like Framlingham between 1970 and 1980 was only just sufficient to increase its real cost of admission. The six fold price increases at sites like Hampton Court and Avebury only represented a 68% increase in real terms. Greater detail for a longer list of sites is given in Tables 8.1 and 8.2.

Table 2.2

Cost of adult admission prices (pence) at selected DoE properties

Site	Admission price	Admission price	Real cost (in 1970 prices)
	1970	1980	1980
Hampton Court	20	120	33.7
Osborne House	20	100	28.1
Audley End	15	100	28.1
Fountains Abbey	15	70	19.7
Dover Castle	10	70	19.7
Stonehenge	10	40	11.2
Housesteads	7.5	60	16.9
Framlingham Castle	7.5	30	8.4
Avebury Museum	5	30	8.4

Table 2.1 shows that the median price at DoE sites changed from the range 1 - 5p in 1970 to the range 21 - 30p in 1980. After the general price rises in 1970, prices remained unchanged at all sites until 1973, when 43 of the 123 sites increased their prices, some by as much as 100%. Prices remained stable in 1974 and, with only 2 exceptions, in 1975. However, in 1976, as a result of Treasury pressure, all but 2 sites raised their prices and 101 of the 123 sites raised prices by 100% or more. Prices were again unchanged in 1977, but were generally raised in 1978, in most cases by between 25% and 50%. In line with the pattern of biennial increases in this period, 1979 was a year of few price changes, but in 1980 most prices were again raised and in a majority of cases the rise was between 75-100%.

It is interesting therefore, that DoE pricing policy, which was determined centrally rather than by the regional offices or the site managers, resulted in very large increases in admission prices at most sites every few years, with little or no change in the intervening years. While administratively convenient, it is likely that this pattern of infrequent but substantial price rises increased initial consumer resistance. We shall return to this point in discussing the results of the analysis presented in Chapter 7.

Since 1978 the overall aim in determining price increases has been to maximise revenue. The distribution of revenue earning capacity is however highly skewed with the ten most popular monuments accounting for approximately 90% of overall revenue and one - the Tower of London - accounting for appproximately 60%.

The National Trust

It is not surprising given the much greater range of facilities available at many National Trust properties and the Trust's decentralised decision making processes, that they tend to display a much greater range of pricing structures than the DoE sites. It is generally true that most National Trust sites have in the past opted for admission charges at the entrance rather than car parking charges. There is however, a wide range of practice on charging for separate facilities within sites. Thus, it is very common for separate charges to be made for admission to house and gardens, and some properties, particularly those with extensive parks, make a separate additional charge for car parking.

The usual pattern of charges is to offer a discount for children and for parties booking in advance. Concessionary rates are not generally offered to pensioners. The majority of properties are closed to the public during the winter months and, where they remain open, it is not generally the policy to offer a lower charge to visitors during this period.

Decisions on revisions to admission prices for individual properties have usually been made by the Trust's regional administrators and local committees in the light of guidance and advice issued by the central administration. Consequently, although prices at any individual property have generally been revised every 2 or 3 years, the aggregate data set shows a fairly gradual increase in average charges over the period studied (Table 2.3).

In the majority of years the average percentage increase did not exceed 18% and real charges have, in most instances, been kept roughly in line with inflation. However, substantial and more widespread increases introduced in 1976, 1978, 1979 and 1980 resulted in admission charges for some sites rising to a level some 40-60% above 1973 prices in real terms. At some of the more popular properties entrance charges have been increased at an above average rate in order to discourage overuse.

Some examples of price changes at particular National Trust sites are given in Table 2.4. This table indicates that while St. Michael's Mount experienced a ten fold price increase between 1970 - 80, this was only a three fold price increase in real terms. At the other end of the spectrum were properties such as Stourhead Gardens, where a more than three fold price increase was not enough to maintain the real value of the admission price after allowing for inflation. Greater detail for a longer list of National Trust sites is given in Tables 8.3 and 8.4.

Table 2.3

Distribution of adult admission prices (pence) at National Trust sites in England and Wales

Years	1-5	6-10	11-20	21-30	31-40	41-50	51-75	76-100	101+	NA
1968	23	32	70	5	-	-	-	-	-	8
1969	32	32	67	5	-	-	-	-	-	13
1970	30	33	67	10	-	-	-	-	-	8
1971	17	33	61	27	4	-	-	-	-	5
1972	12	30	60	35	5	-	-	-	-	6
1973	8	23	55	44	10	2	-	-	-	6
1974	8	19	42	45	20	8	-	-	-	6
1975	6	17	33	45	26	11	4	-	-	6
1976	-	10	20	27	32	20	26	6	-	7
1977	-	7	16	21	21	30	36	10	1	6
1978	-	-	15	15	23	29	35	20	1	9
1979	-	-	12	7	13	26	46	36	1	7
1980	-	-	5	10	5	12	32	41	25	4

In many instances National Trust admission charges have been set at a level which is likely to encourage visitors to become members of the Trust. In recent years this implicit policy has been backed up by a vigorous recruitment campaign designed to draw visitors' attention to the potential advantages of membership.

It can be seen from Table 2.3 that median charges at National Trust sites rose from 11-20p in 1968 to 76-100p in 1980. This table highlights the much higher charges at National Trust sites relative to those at DoE sites. In part this can be attributed to the size and range of facilities at typical National Trust properties. It can also be seen from Table 2.3 that there is a much wider dispersion of prices around the median for National Trust properties than for the DoE sites included in Table 2.1. This was the case throughout the period 1970-1980. It is not clear to what extent this reflects the diversity of National Trust sites relative to DoE sites and to what extent it can be explained by a greater willingness on the part of the National Trust's regional administrators to tailor price levels more closely to the relative attractions and operating costs of individual properties.

Table 2.4

Cost of adult admission price (pence) at selected National Trust properties

Site	Admission price 1970	Admission price 1980	Real cost (in 1970 prices) 1980*
Waddesdon Manor	30	140	39.3
Hardwick Hall	30	120	33.7
Hidcote Manor Gardens	25	110	30.9
Stourhead Gardens	25	80	22.5
Wallington	20	120	33.7
Packwood House	20	85	23.9
St. Michael's Mount	10	100	28.1
Shugborough	10	50	14.0
Tatton Gardens	5	30	8.4

In each year a significant number of sites changed their price and this contrasts strongly with the pattern identified earlier for DoE properties. The years in which the largest and most widespread price changes occurred (1970, 1976 and 1980) were all years in which general resource constraints were experienced in the public sector. However, it is worth noting that in the period from 1970-1980, there were 175 instances of DoE sites increasing admission charges for sites by over 75% but only 72 instances of National Trust properties for which this occurred. This tendency for National Trust properties to increase prices more smoothly than DoE sites has been even more pronounced since 1977; from 1977 to 1980, there were 73 instances of DoE properties increasing their prices by over 50%, but only 23 instances of this occurring for National Trust properties.

Local authorities

Local authorities, in their management of country parks, have the legal power to make charges for car parking and for most facilities provided specifically for visitors; they do not appear, however, to have the legal power to charge for admission to the parks themselves. Two thirds of country parks do, in practice, make some kind of car park or facility charge and over half of these have car parking charges. Naturally, charges are mainly applied at sites which provide visitor attractions or facilities, especially those relating to active recreation; only one third of sites offering purely passive recreation make charges (Countryside Commission 1979a).

Private operators

Most private members of the Historic Houses Association charge either an all-inclusive admission price or give a choice of one price for house and garden and another price for gardens. Very few charge separately for individual facilities within the site, although some of the very large properties such as Chatsworth do this. It is quite common for admission prices for children to be as low as 25% of those for adults or as high as 70%. Higher admission prices for children tend to occur where the properties have especially vulnerable contents and relatively lower prices tend to be charged for admission to gardens and parkland.

Charges for admission to houses in the private sector were approximately 10p above those for comparable National Trust properties in 1977 (Lees and Coyne 1979). By 1980, however, it appears that National Trust properties had actually increased charges to levels above those of comparable private operators (English Tourist Board 1981). Lees and Coyne argue that the financial resources of the National Trust and local authorities free them from the need to rely on admissions revenue alone and therefore allow them to pursue pricing policies which act as an effective check on any tendency for private sites to set excessive charges. They go on to argue, however,that most private properties were not able to cover costs (in 1978) from admission and ancillary income. Indeed, Butler (1981) has estimated that no more than 20 - 30 historic houses earn enough in visitor income to support the mansion, including provision for major repairs. As National Trust admission prices would now appear to have caught up with private charges, it would be interesting to trace the relative changes in admissions to the two classes of property since 1981 and to analyse the complementary changes in pricing structure which some National Trust properties might consider to protect themselves from the increased private sector competition.

Summary and conclusions

Wide variations in charging practices have been identified between the DoE, National Trust, local authorities and private operators. This applies to practices on both the level and the structure of charges. It is not clear that these differences arise from explicitly defined differences in objectives or differences in operating conditions. The implications of these variations in practice are explored in later chapters.

3 Trends in visits

Overall trends in visits to historic properties in the countryside

Since the 1950's the number of visits to the countryside for recreation purposes has increased substantially. The analysis reported by Stoakes (1979) indicates that the increase in the number of paying visitors to National Trust properties was around 7% per annum from 1955 to 1974 (Figure 3.1). For Department of Environment properties in the period from 1968 to 1972, growth in admissions was about 10% per annum. However, in both cases these trends appear to have disappeared after the 1973-74 period. Changes in the total number of paying visitors to a sample of DoE and National Trust sites during the period from 1973 to 1980 are shown in Figures 3.2 and 3.3. The sample consists in each case of all sites for which complete data were available over the period.

DoE Sites

It can be seen that visits to DoE sites fell sharply in 1974, 1976 and (in the case of the larger sites for which data was available) in 1979 and 1980. The total number of paying admissions has not regained its 1973 level since that time (Table 3.1).

Increases in admission prices probably contributed to this decline in the number of paying visitors. It is interesting to note, however, that the major price increases which were introduced in 1973, 1976, 1978 and 1980 were not consistently reflected in changes in the total number of visitors to DoE sites (Figure 3.2).

National Trust Sites

The pre 1973 growth trend also appears to have disappeared in the case of National Trust sites (Figure 3.3). The sharp burst of growth in 1978 brought visitor levels to a new peak but by 1980 the number of paying visitors had fallen below the 1971 level (Table 3.1). Comparison of Figures 3.2 and 3.3 indicates that visitor numbers to DoE sites have been subject to wider variations from year to year than National Trust sites. Evidence discussed in Chapters 6 and 7 suggests that in part this may be due to the DoE's practice of introducing larger but less frequent price increases than the National Trust.

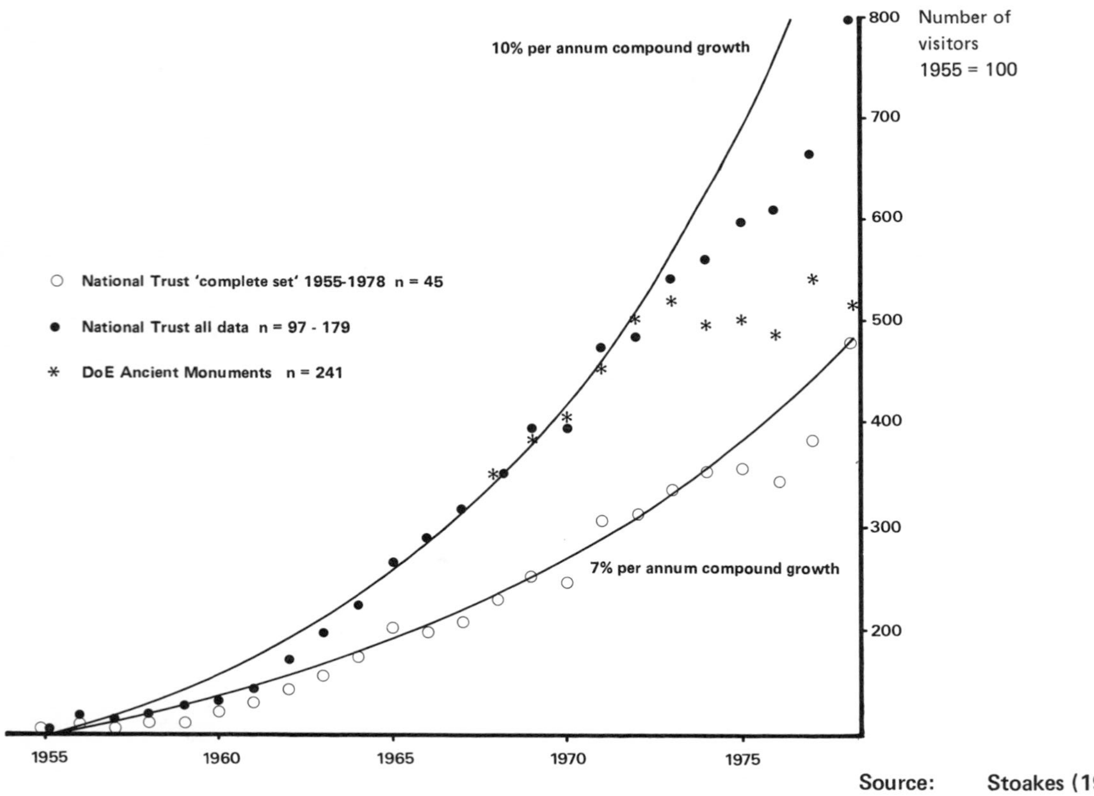

Source: Stoakes (1982)

Figure 3.1 Growth in number of visitors to National Trust and DoE sites

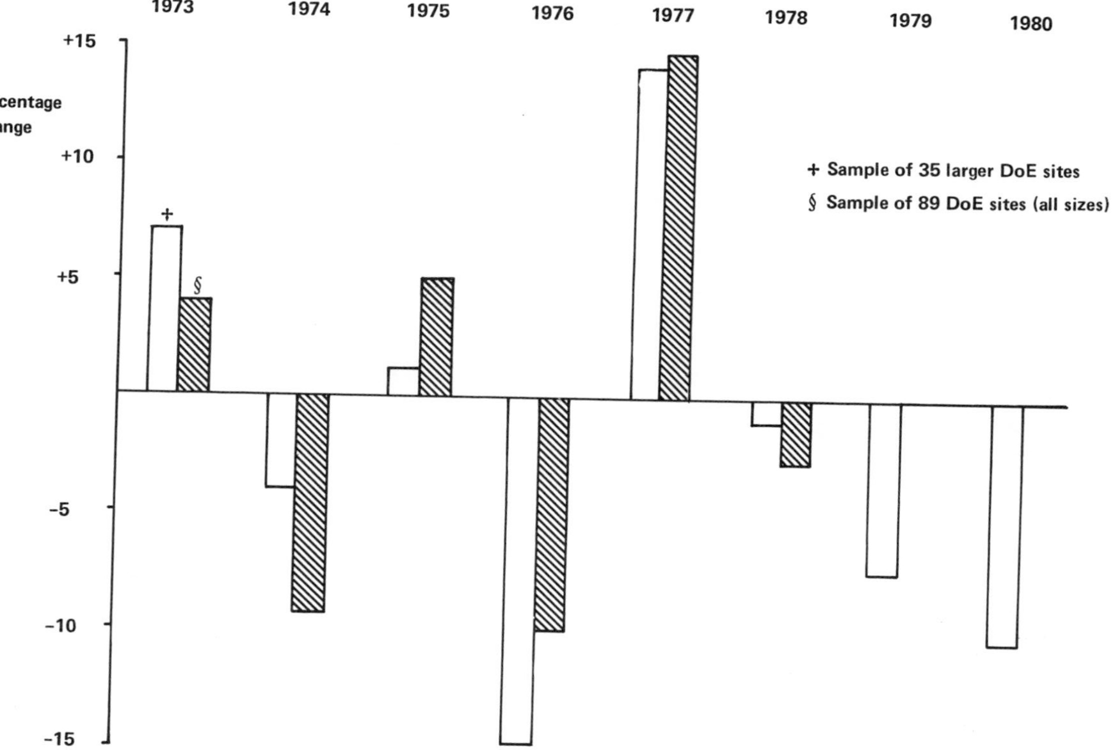

Figure 3.2 Annual percentage change in the number of paying visitors to DoE sites in England

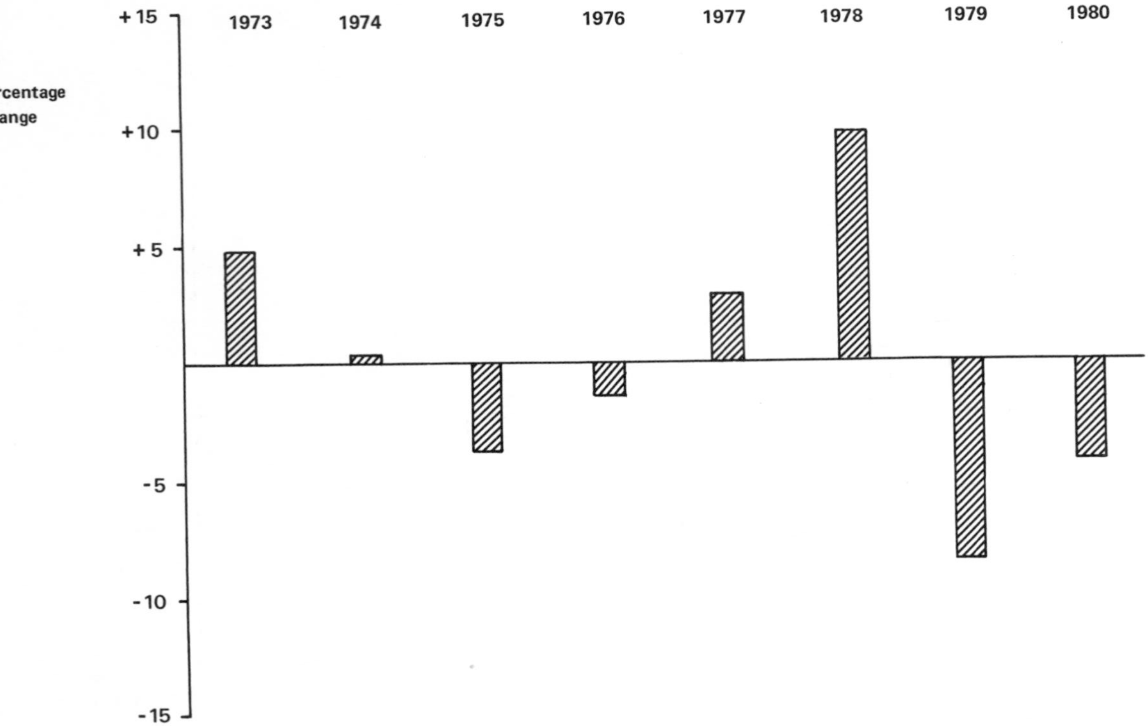

Figure 3.3 Annual percentage change in the number of paying visitors to National Trust sites in England and Wales

Table 3.1

Trends in the number of paying visitors (full rate)

Year	DoE sites		National Trust sites
	All sites	Larger sites	
1968	-	-	2,270,297
1969	-	-	2,440,794
1970	-	-	2,331,376
1971	-	-	2,748,778
1972	5,046,432	2,082,281	2,679,902
1973	5,246,832	2,244,967	2,808,438
1974	4,769,551	2,154,130	2,827,371
1975	5,006,731	2,182,630	2,725,466
1976	4,512,833	1,859,392	2,648,012
1977	5,154,137	2,134,095	2,761,265
1978	5,019,255	2,113,589	3,029,337
1979	-	1,956,575	2,774,424
1980	-	1,756,298	2,656,840

Trends by ownership and region

The figures in Table 3.2, which have been extracted from the English Heritage Monitor, are based on a constant sample of sites over the period from 1975 to 1980. They show that, while DoE properties experienced a drop of 12% in visitors over this period, National Trust properties had an increase of 32% (although admissions of non-members fell by 3%) and private properties an increase of 9%. During this period admission prices for DoE properties certainly increased fastest, but price rises at National Trust and private properties seem to have been at similar rates, at least from 1977 to 1980 (English Heritage Monitor 1981, p. 23). The difference in admission trends cannot therefore be attributed to changes in admission prices alone.

Table 3.2 also illustrates the wide deviations in visitor trends between regions. At one end of the spectrum, properties in Northumbria experienced a decline of 15% over the 1975-1980 period whilst, at the other end, properties in the East Midlands gained 15%. These variations point to the need for a more systematic and detailed regional analysis of visitor trends (see also Appendix A).

Countryside recreation and the economy

The sharp break in 1974 from the previous steady growth trend in countryside recreation trips presents a dilemma. Is the era of growth now over; or has the

Table 3.2

Visitor trends by ownership and region

Tourist Board Region	% change in the number of visitors 1975-80			
	DoE properties	National Trust properties	Private properties	All properties
Cumbria	-33	+29	+24	+8
Northumbria	-23	+8	-11	-15
North West	+11	+13	-	+12
Yorkshire	-16	+37	+4	-3
Heart of England	-19	+38	-	-
East Midlands	-23	+23	+32	+15
Thames and Chilterns	-12	+19	-9	-7
East Anglia	-17	+26	+18	+7
London	-4	+4	-19	+1
West Country	-7	+52	+6	+12
Southern	-24	+32	+28	+6
South East	-28	+29	+28	+13
England	-12	+32	+9	+4

Sources: English Heritage Monitor 1981 (English Tourist Board, from DoE, National Trust and ETB/Daily Telegraph sources).

Note: National Trust figures include admissions by members and non-members.

post-1973 pattern been merely a temporary deviation from the long-term trend? To answer these questions it is necessary to explore the influence on countryside recreation behaviour of the major economic and social changes which have occurred since 1973 and the extent to which these changes in turn may be permanent or merely cyclical.

After several decades of believing in the inevitability of economic growth, the economic stability of the world was severely jolted by the 1973-74 Arab oil embargo. The immediate effects on Britain were seen in a trebling of oil prices and for a few months there were actual shortages at filling stations. The oil price rise had a two fold impact on travel costs and on economic activity generally.

Petrol prices

Whilst much publicity was given to the rise in petrol prices in the 1970's, the rise in petrol prices in real terms (after allowing for inflation) was much slower and more erratic. Indeed, from 1975 the real price of petrol actually fell and by 1978 it was almost back to its 1973 level (Figure 3.4).

For most visitors, accessibility to the countryside depends on car ownership as well as the cost of running a car. The steady growth of car ownership since 1957 is illustrated in Table 3.3; the effect of petrol price increases is seen only in a temporary halt to the trend in 1974. Car ownership therefore, would not appear to have imposed a significant constraint on countryside recreation, even after 1973. Nonetheless, the effect of higher real petrol prices in 1974-75 and again in 1979-80 gives rise to the expectation that fewer and shorter trips might be undertaken. As Table 3.3 shows, this does appear to have happened in the 1974-76 period, but not in the 1978-80 period.

Table 3.3

Car ownership and inland private road passenger kilometres travelled (UK)

Year	Inland private road passenger km ('000m)	Private cars currently licensed
1957	112	4.2m
1965	233	8.9m
1973	364	13.5m
1974	350	13.7m
1976	367	14.1m
1978	412	14.2m
1980	433	15.2m

Source: Annual Abstract of Statistics, 1967, 1975, 1982.

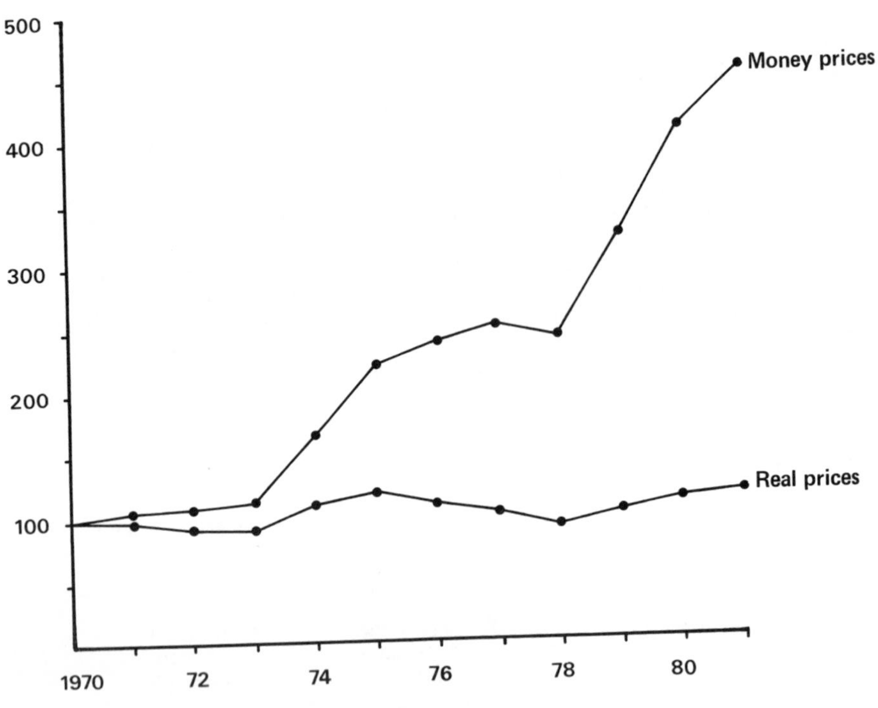

Figure 3.4 Indices of change in petrol prices 1970-81

More direct evidence on changes in countryside tripmaking comes from comparison of the results of the Countryside Commission's National Survey of Countryside Recreation in 1977 (a boom year) and 1980 (a slump year, with higher real petrol prices). Stoakes (1982) shows that between 1977 and 1980 there was a significant increase (from 46% to 58%) in the number of people making no countryside trip at all in the four weeks prior to interview (Table 3.4). He concludes that the main effect of changing economic circumstances between the 'boom' year of 1977 and the slump year of 1980 was a reduction in the number of people participating rather than a change in the frequency of participation among participants - implying that people tended to stop making such trips altogether rather than scale down their level of activity.

Table 3.4

Distribution of total day trips to countryside in four weeks prior to interview

	1977		1980	
	% of sample	% of total trips	% of sample	% of total trips
0 trips	46	0	58	0
1-8 trips	46	52	33	54
Over 8 trips	7	48	6	46
Not known	1	0	3	0
Average frequency		4.2		4.7

Source: Stoakes (1982)

From the same surveys it is possible to ascertain whether trip lengths decreased between these years. The results show only minor changes in trip lengths for all categories of trip other than day trips from home while on holiday (Table 3.5).

Changes in accessibility, whether due to changes in car ownership or petrol costs, do not therefore, seem to provide a convincing explanation for the downward trend in countryside recreation trips referred to at the beginning of this chapter, although large increases in petrol prices do appear to have had short-term effects.

Economic recession

The oil crisis in 1973 was followed by an international recession which broke the long post-war record of employment and income growth in Western Europe and

North America. After a halting recovery in 1977-78, international recession returned in 1979-80. As a result, the rate of growth of national income (GDP) and consumer expenditure within the United Kingdom fell markedly, whilst unemployment rose from 2.6% in 1973 to 6.7% in 1980 (Figure 3.5).

The period since 1973 has not been one of unrelieved gloom. The period from 1975-77 saw a growth in GDP, but almost all of this was in stock building and increased exports, while consumer expenditure actually fell marginally. In the next two years up to 1979, GDP grew slightly less (at about 2-3% per annum) but this largely took the form of a dramatic burst of consumer expenditure. This was the only period since 1973 when real wages did not fall or at best remain static. Unemployment rose steadily over most of the period except for a brief respite in 1978 and 1979 when it declined slightly.

If we compare the changes in the economic indices illustrated in Figure 3.5 with changes in admissions, illustrated in Figure 3.3, it is clear that there is a strong correspondence between trends in consumer expenditure and trends in admissions to National Trust properties. The correspondence with trends in admissions to DoE properties is very much weaker (Figure 3.2) and the fall in admissions in 1978 appears to present a major anomaly, given the large increases in consumer expenditure and the marked rise in National Trust admissions in that year. This particular anomaly may be partially due to the higher price increases at DoE properties as compared with National Trust properties in 1978. However, the complexity of the overall picture once again emphasises that crude comparisons of annual figures of admissions and other aggregate variables (such as national income, expenditure or unemployment) cannot give reliable explanations of variations in demand. The more detailed econometric approach described in Chapters 6 - 8 assesses the influence of these various factors together, rather than one at a time, in order to provide a more systematic picture of the influence they have had on visitor trends.

Table 3.5

Average distance (km.) of day trips to countryside (excluding walkers and riders)

Origin of trip	1977	1980
Long holiday	42.5	45.2
Short holiday	53.9	51.6
At home on holiday	65.9	57.4
Home	53.5	49.7
Average for all trips	53.2	50.1

Source: Stoakes (1982)

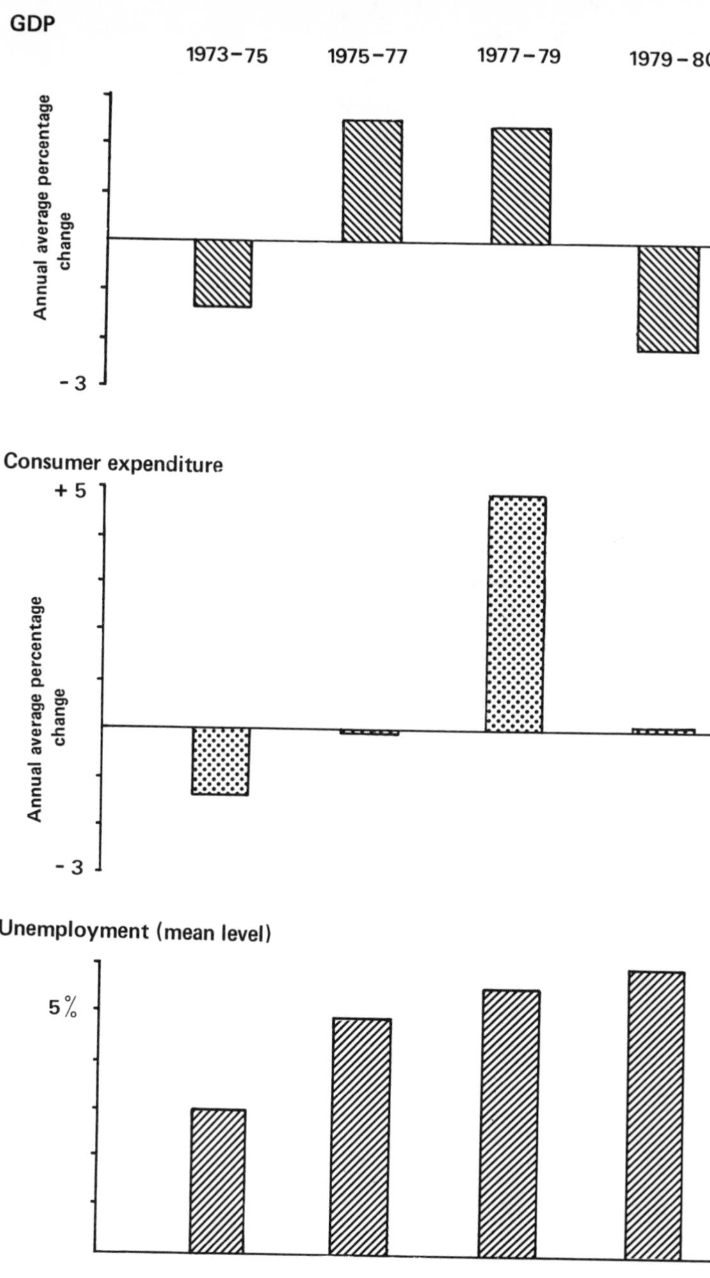

Source: Economic Trends; Economic Progress Report

Figure 3.5 Change in selected macroeconomic variables in the UK economy 1973-80

Tourism and holidays away from home

The 1977 and 1980 National Surveys of Countryside Recreation carried out by the Countryside Commission show the importance of trips made while on holiday in the total volume of countryside trips (Table 3.6).

Table 3.6

Number of countryside recreation trips (millions) made in average summer month

Year	Total trips	From home	Whilst away on holiday
1977	100	65	35
1980	81	62	19

Source: Stoakes (1982)

It is also clear from Table 3.6 that the 19% overall reduction in countryside trips between 1977 and 1980 is largely accounted for by the 46% decline in trips made from a holiday base. In contrast, day trips from home declined by only 5% during this period. Since the average number of trips made by households whilst on holiday declined only from 5.7 to 5.5 the fall in the volume of holiday trips was essentially due to the decline in the number of households taking holidays away from home from 25% of the sample in 1977 to 15% in 1980.

Day trips to the countryside appear to have been relatively insensitive to increased travel costs and worsening national economic conditions during this period. However, Stoakes (1982) points out that these figures may be masking a more complex set of changes in which those people who made fewer holiday trips may have made some day trips to compensate and in doing so they may have masked reductions in day trip making as others reacted to increases in travel costs and the economic downturn.

The balance between holidays spent away from home in Britain and at home therefore appears to be a major determinant of changes in the volume of countryside recreation trip making. This balance is affected by the overall level of activity in the economy; for example, holidays of four or more nights away from home by British residents increased by 10% in 1978. The split between holidays at home and holidays abroad is further influenced by the foreign exchange rate. The fall in the exchange rate from 1974 to 1977 was therefore associated with lower average numbers of holidays abroad and the rising exchange rate from 1978 to 1980 saw holidays abroad rise to 53% above the 1977 level (British National Travel Survey 1981). Upward movements in the exchange rate have also tended to reduce the volume of foreign visitors to

Britain, which in turn has also reduced visits to historic buildings and, to a much lesser degree, overall visits to the countryside.

Pricing policy and visitor trends

Can the increases in real admission prices to many countryside facilities described in Chapter 2, be blamed for the fall-off in trips in the 1970's? It does seem likely that admission prices have played an increasingly important role in the decision whether or not to make a trip and where to go. If we consider the costs incurred by a typical party of two adults and two children, petrol and admission charges are the main items. Table 3.7 is compiled on the assumption of a 30 mile round trip (the average length of trips to National Trust properties for parties with children interviewed in recent visitor surveys) petrol consumption of 30 miles per gallon and half price admission for children. It shows that party admission costs have risen much more quickly than petrol prices since 1974 for visitors both to DoE and National Trust sites. Indeed, for visitors to National Trust properties (and by implication, to private properties since their admission prices are now broadly in line with National Trust prices) admission costs have come to dominate total trip costs since 1974. For DoE sites, typical party admission costs may still only account for about 36% of total trip costs, but this proportion has risen from 18% in 1974.

Table 3.7

Comparison of typical trip petrol costs and party admission costs 1970-1980

	Typical adult admission costs		Typical party admission costs		Petrol costs per gallon
	DoE	NT	DoE	NT	
1970	3p	12p	9p	36p	30p
1974	4p	20p	12p	60p	55p
1977	8p	45p	24p	135p	84p
1980	25p	75p	75p	225p	135p

The evidence discussed above that average trip lengths have not fallen substantially for the reduced number of households who still regularly make countryside recreation trips suggests that, once the decision is taken to undertake a trip, the choice of destination is not decided mainly on the basis of travel costs (either petrol or travel time costs). This accords with the suggestion that there may be a minimum distance for a trip before a household

Table 3.8

Expected relationship between changes in number of visitors and changes in admission prices at a sample of sites in a year

% Change in admission prices	Number of sites experiencing % change in number of paying visitors						
	Decrease over 20%	Decrease 11-20%	Decrease Up to 10%	No change	Increase up to 10%	Increase 11-20%	Increase over 20%
Decrease	-	-	-	-	-	5	-
No change	-	-	-	-	10	-	-
Increase up to 10%	-	-	-	20	-	-	-
Increase 11-30%	-	-	60	-	-	-	-
Increase 31-50%	-	25	-	-	-	-	-
Increase over 50%	5	-	-	-	-	-	-

Table 3.9

Actual relationship between changes in number of visitors and changes in admission prices at a sample of DoE sites in 1978

% Change in admission prices	Number of sites experiencing % Change in number of paying visitors						
	Decrease over 20%	Decrease 11-20%	Decrease up to 10%	No change	Increase up to 10%	Increase 11-20%	Increase over 20%
Decrease	-	-	1	-	-	-	-
No change	2	1	2	-	1	1	-
Increase up to 10%	-	-	-	-	-	-	-
Increase 11-30%	-	-	8	1	5	1	-
Increase 31-50%	7	13	30	7	13	8	5
Increase over 50%	-	-	3	-	-	-	-

feels that it has 'got away' into the countryside. This implies that although petrol costs and admission costs together may have an important influence on household decisions whether or not to make a trip, the decision on which destination to visit may be dominated by admission prices, quality of facilities, amenities etc.. This is all the more likely since admission costs have come to represent a much higher proportion of total trip costs (Table 3.7).

In addition, the phenomenon of rising real admission prices has coincided with (and been partly because of) the economic downturn since 1973. This may be expected to have made visitors more sensitive to admission prices, especially between different types of properties and individual sites with differing pricing policies. Setting the right price, in the context of the competition in the market, has probably therefore become more important since the mid-1970's.

It is not, however, appropriate to make a blanket judgement that increases in real admission prices will bring significant reductions in admissions to facilities. As has been stressed earlier in this chapter, there are many complex factors, often interacting, which exert an influence on visitor trends. Using simple rules of thumb may often lead to highly inaccurate forecasts of the results of policies. This can be vividly demonstrated by looking at the changes in the number of visits to DoE sites, broken down by the extent of price increases. We would expect a pattern where - the higher the price increase, the bigger the fall in admissions (Table 3.8). In practice, the range of changes in the number of visits for each group of sites with similar price changes can be very wide indeed. For example, two DoE sites which did not change their price in 1978 lost over 20% of their visitors (Table 3.9). When all the 83 sites which increased prices by between 31% and 50% are studied, we find their experiences ranged from 7 sites with more than a 20% decrease in admissions, 30 sites with a decrease of up to 10% and 26 sites with an increase in admissions (5 of which had more than a 20% increase). Similar breakdowns for DoE and National Trust properties from 1969 - 1979 are given in Appendix C.

Summary and conclusions

The foregoing discussion of the effects of petrol costs, national income, consumer expenditure and patterns of holiday making does not suggest clear-cut and entirely reliable relationships between changes in such aggregate variables and changes in the number of countryside recreation trips. The strongest relationship appears to be between changes in the number of countryside recreation trips and changes in the number of holidays away from home in Britain. This is to a large extent dependent on the state of the economy, which also affects countryside trip making through the influence on consumer expenditure. While increases in real petrol costs appear to have short-term effects, their longer-term influence on countryside trip making is less clear, especially as the range of variation of real petrol costs has not actually been very large over the period studied.

The evidence suggests that many households have greatly reduced the frequency of their countryside recreation trips, or holidays away from home which so often entail such trips. The remaining households have, if anything increased their frequency of trips and have not substantially decreased trip lengths. For those continuing to make countryside recreation trips, the willingness to pay clearly remains even though, as seems likely, their ability to pay may have been squeezed. For those who have dropped out of countryside trip making, diminished ability to pay would seem to have been a major cause. Indeed, Stoakes (1982) shows that lower social groups have tended to display the largest fall-off in countryside trip making. In addition, some switch to cheaper facilities (urban attractions closer to home, holidays abroad when the exchange rate is favourable) seems to have occurred when the price differentials have widened sufficiently.

It is clear, however, that to establish the full significance of the influence of pricing policy on the visitor trends outlined in this chapter, aggregate analysis of changes in the total number of visits between years for DoE, National Trust or other sites is not adequate. Rather, a detailed analysis of the effects of changes in admission prices on countryside visits is necessary which also takes account of changes in the economy, in the weather and in the supply side of the market. This is the rationale for the econometric analysis developed in the next two chapters.

4 Demand for countryside recreation facilities

Introduction

As we have seen in Chapter 3, admission price is only one of a range of factors which people may consider before deciding to visit a specific countryside recreation site. If we are to clarify the true effect of site pricing policies, we must know about and take full account of the other important factors. Obviously, many such factors might be considered; in this chapter those factors which can be expected to apply to a wide range of sites are discussed. In addition to exploring the factors influencing demand, the responses which site managers are able to make to control or change demand are examined. The next chapter describes ways in which the actual importance of these factors, including variations in admission prices, can be estimated.

Influences on countryside recreation trips

Understanding the influence of factors which can be most easily used by site managers to influence demand is obviously especially important. In order to identify these factors, it is desirable to split the analysis into two parts:

(i) Analysis of factors which may influence the decision to make a recreational trip to the countryside, and

(ii) Analysis of factors which may influence the decision to visit particular sites or facilities while on this trip.

Some people will make these decisions simultaneously; others may make the decision on which particular site to visit after deciding to undertake a recreational trip (Elson 1979; Hensher 1979). These two different starting points may lead to important differences in visitor behaviour.

A concise survey of English and American research on the factors which are likely to influence people who are considering whether or not to make a countryside recreational trip, is given by Elson (1979). A critical review of existing models of recreational travel is contained in TRRU (1980). The four main factors influencing demand for countryside trips, as alternatives to other recreation or leisure activities, identified by these two reviews are:

(i) accessibility

(ii) 'affordability'

(iii) preferences

(iv) weather.

Of these, the first three factors are intrinsic to the countryside recreation facilities actually available; the fourth factor is extrinsic to the facilities but affects both their demand and supply. The way in which these factors are hypothesised to relate to each other is set out in Figure 4.1.

(i) Accessibility

The accessibility of countryside recreation facilities depends on distance, on transport availability (especially car availability), on money costs of travelling and time spent in travelling. Although this implies that more remote countryside facilities are likely to have lower demand, this may not be the case if the route taken is itself interesting (Miles and Smith 1977) or if time spent travelling within the broad destination zone is a large proportion of the overall trip (TRRU 1980). Moreover, it has been suggested that a certain minimum distance may be accepted in order to feel that one has 'got away' (Bonsey 1968). Nevertheless, it is clear that, in general, distance does deter trip making.

(ii) 'Affordability'

'Affordability' relates the sum of the prices paid by visitors at sites and the travel costs of getting there to the income levels of the visitors. When these costs rise relative to incomes, the demand for countryside trips can be expected to fall.

(iii) Preferences

Individual and household preferences for countryside trips rather than other activities, such as urban trips or staying at home, will affect demand both between social groups and over time. These preferences will partly reflect perceptions of the relative quality of available opportunities for countryside and urban recreation. There is also substantial evidence that low income households are less likely to make countryside recreation trips than high and middle income households (Countryside Commission 1981). Of course, household preferences are subject to short-term changes as a result of fashion, media publicity and site promotion, as well as caprice. However, preferences are also subject to longer-term changes in the household's age range, structure and changing interests and capacities.

We might characterize the preferences factor as determining the household's 'willingness to pay' for countryside recreation trips, against other uses of its income; while 'affordability' means the household's 'ability to pay'. As we argued in Chapter 3, recent trends in visitor numbers have been influenced more by changes in ability to pay than by changes in willingness to pay for countryside recreation trips.

TOTAL POPULATION

Composition of population in terms of attributes relevant to recreation behaviour

e.g.

number of families with young children, number of socio-economic groups A and B, number of households with high educational qualifications, number of car owners etc..

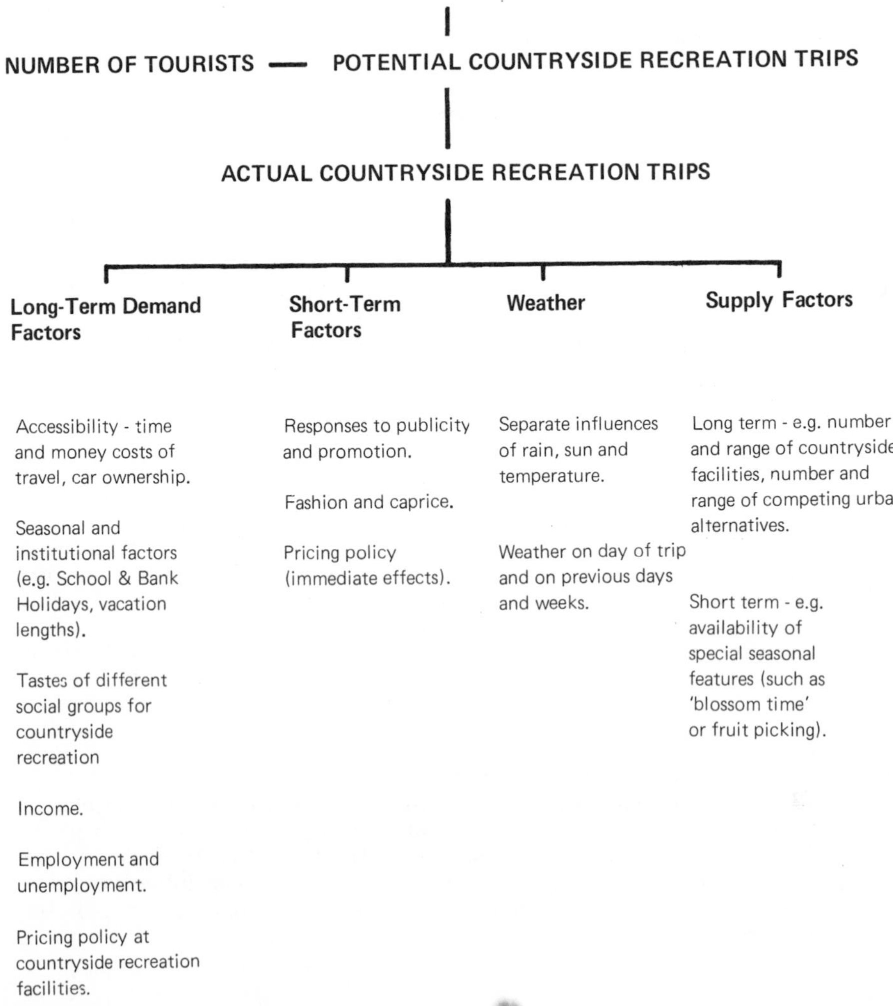

Figure 4.1

Influences on the number of recreational trips to the countryside from a given population

(iv) Weather

The choice between urban and countryside trips and, indeed, the decision on whether or not to make any recreational trip at all, is likely to be highly influenced by the weather. This is an area where recreation managers tend to have rather loose and often conflicting impressions based on experience rather than firm knowledge; academic studies have not explored in detail the effects of weather on recreation in Britain. Questions as to whether the important variable is the weather in the week or the day before a trip, or the weather on the actual day of the trip; the relative importance of rain, sunshine and temperature and the relative weight given to weather at the origin and the destination of a trip therefore remain largely unresolved. Whatever the volatile pattern of the weather in a particular area, average weather conditions over a number of years also play a part in determining the sort of facilities which trip makers frequent. Facilities which are fair-weather in character will therefore experience different demand responses in the different weather regions of the country.

This list of factors refers to the considerations influencing an individual or family making the decision whether or not to visit the countryside. The total number of trips made to the countryside depends, therefore, on all these factors and also, of course, on trends in the numbers of individuals and families who are in a position to make this choice. For most recreation facilities, this means that demographic factors within their catchment areas are important. However, a proportion of countryside recreation trips each year is made by tourists, and their number each year is therefore a further factor influencing aggregate visits to the countryside. For the purposes of this study the factors which affect the decision by tourists whether or not to make countryside recreational trips are assumed to be similar in nature, if rather different in balance, to those affecting the decisions of United Kingdom residents.

The taste factors which determine long-term demand by different social groups can be applied to the numbers in each social group to calculate the 'potential countryside recreation trips' (Fitton 1979). The extent to which these are translated into actual trips will depend upon the supply factors, the weather variables and the other long and short-term demand factors included in Figure 4.1. This is, of course, a very crude model of how such decisions are made in practice, but it is helpful when discussing the possible ways of estimating the short and long-term effects of pricing policy on actual visits to sites.

Influences on visits to particular sites

In attempting to identify the factors which influence the proportion of countryside visitors who make trips to particular sites, we are essentially concerned with factors which affect the 'market share' which each site is able to obtain. As with any private sector organisation, market share can be expected to be directly affected by the relative position of the site as compared to its competitors. The eight main factors which site managers can influence in order to improve the competitive position of their sites are:

(i) Pricing policy (perceived value for money)

(ii) Uniqueness or unusual combinations of facilities/attractions

(iii) Changing or additonal attractions

(iv) 'Image' relative to other countryside facilities/attractions

(v) Accessibility to a large percentage of the potential market

(vi) Awareness by the public of the site's existence and characteristics

(vii) Visitor perceptions of what is available

(viii) Weather dependency of the site.

We can therefore expect that the proportion of total visits which go to a particular site will be influenced by its location in relation to competing attractions, the number and quality of those competing attractions and the site's attractiveness relative to its competition, as measured against factors (i) - (viii) above.

What can site managers do to influence demand?

Managers of individual sites can only attempt to influence demand at their own site. They can do this by creating extra demand for countryside trips which would not otherwise have existed or by diverting demand from their competitors' sites to their own sites.

If we examine the above list of factors affecting demand for visits to individual sites, we see that a number are within the control or influence of site managers, to a greater or lesser degree. At one end of the spectrum, the location of the site and the location and quality of competing sites are given factors, once the site has been provided. At the other end of the spectrum, site managers (or their controlling agencies) have discretion over site promotion. Pricing policy is generally also an area where site managers have control, although it is sometimes subject to some constraints imposed by legislation or legal covenants. In the longer term it will often be possible for site managers to take steps to add to the attractiveness of a site by incorporating unique features, by continually changing or adding attractions, by reducing the site's dependence on good weather and by raising the expectations of visitors by establishing a high level of goodwill with new and regular visitors.

In deciding how to change the 'product' in these ways, it is necessary to understand the characteristics of demand for the site. This entails monitoring the separate effects of each of the factors which may influence demand. The next chapter considers how this may be done.

Summary and conclusions

Admission prices and charging structure are just two of the variables which influence demand for visits to countryside recreation sites. They may or may not be important in particular circumstances. Even when admission price appears to be of minor significance compared to other variables, however, there is a need for care in setting the right price at a site since competing facilities generally offer a wide choice to trip makers. More importantly, however, price and charging structure are directly under the control of site managers and can be changed far more quickly than most of the other factors affecting demand. This means that it is particularly valuable to know more about the precise effects of admission prices on the pattern of demand.

5 Practical approaches to estimating the effect of admission prices on demand

Introduction

In order to identify the effect of admission prices on demand for visits to countryside recreation sites, it is necessary to control for the influence of the other important variables discussed in Chapter 4. In view of the wide range of these variables and the difficulties in identifying and quantifying their influences, 'guestimates' based on the experience of site managers are especially likely to be inaccurate. Consequently some more precise method of sorting out the separate influences of different factors is needed. This chapter discusses how available data may be analysed in order to achieve more precise estimates of price elasticity. A more detailed discussion of data sources and the statistical analyses which may be used to estimate demand functions can be found in Appendix A.

Data requirements

The relationship between changes in admission prices and changes in numbers of visits to sites can be estimated from data of two main types:

(i) 'Time series' data

The sensitivity of visits to a particular site to changes in admission prices can be estimated from a series of measures of visits and prices over a period of time during which real and/or money prices have varied significantly.

(ii) 'Cross-sectional' data

If admission prices or changes in admission prices have varied <u>between</u> sites, it is also possible to estimate the elasticity of demand from data relating to shorter periods of time by correlating changes in the level of prices with changes in the number of visits for a 'cross-section' of sites.

In practice, the choice of which method to use will obviously be governed by data availability. Both methods, however, require fairly detailed analysis of disaggregated data in order to disentangle the possible effects of changes in admission prices from the wide range of other intrinsic and extrinsic factors which may influence visits to particular sites.

Data sources

A major objective of the present study was to provide guidance for local authorities and other site operators on appropriate levels of charges and their likely effects on visitor use at country parks. Unfortunately, however, because of the relative novelty of such facilities and the often unsophisticated methods which have been used to collect charges at such sites, reliable data on the number of visitors to country parks was extremely limited. In the long term this gap in basic information will be bridged for a sample of sites by the management information data bank which the Countryside Commission proposes to establish with the co-operation of local authorities, the National Trust, Department of Environment and private operators. In the present study, however, it was necessary to concentrate attention on analogous sites administered by the National Trust and the Department of the Environment for which longer and more reliable time series data were already available or could be assembled.

For both categories of site the data on visitor numbers is produced as a by-product of accounting procedures rather than for any specific site management purposes. In our analysis particular attention was focussed on those sites which are officially recognised country parks operated by the National Trust and those which include substantial areas of open land for informal recreation.

Nature of the data

The data used in the statistical analyses described in subsequent chapters included not only details of admission prices and the number of visits to individual sites, but also information on site characteristics and weather conditions. The kind of data included on the data card for each site is illustrated in Figure 5.1.

Admission prices and visits

Data on admission prices and the number of visits to the sites included in the analysis comprised:

(i) Annual data on admission charges and the total number of visits to National Trust and DoE sites from 1970 to 1980,

(ii) Monthly data on admission charges and numbers of visits to a 'sample' of National Trust and DoE sites.

The data for each site were checked and anomalies corrected where possible by referring to the records of site managers. In the small number of cases where remaining problems may have influenced the results described in later chapters, attention has been drawn to the nature and extent of the probable influence.

Site characteristics

Each of the sites included in the analyses was classified according to its location and its type. The characteristics covered in this classification included:

SITE :

SITE :

SITE :

LOCATION

URBAN ☐
URBAN/FRINGE ☐
URBAN INFLUENCED ☐
RURAL ☐

NATIONAL PARK ☐

HOLIDAY AREA ☐

TYPE

HOUSE☐ CASTLE☐ ABBEY☐ PRIORY☐ ARCH'L☐
GARDEN☐ PARK☐

YEAR	PRICE	VISITORS	TEMP	SUN	RAIN
1970					
1971					
1972					
1973					
1974					
1975					
1976					
1977					
1978					
1979					
1980					

Figure 5.1 **Data availability for sites included in the statistical analysis**

(i) Location - urban, urban fringe, urban influenced, rural, within National Park and/or recognised holiday area and

(ii) Type - house, castle, abbey, priory, archeological site, garden, park.

Weather data

Data on local weather conditions derived from published and unpublished Meteorological Office sources were added to the record for each site. The weather data used included variables for temperature, sunshine and rainfall.

Types of analysis

In order to identify the principal factors which have influenced changes in the number of visits to these sites three forms of analysis were carried out:

(i) Cross-sectional analysis

(ii) Longitudinal analysis

(iii) Time series analysis

Cross-sectional analysis

The cross-sectional analysis involved comparing variations in admission prices and the number of visitors between specific periods across all the sites in order to obtain a 'cross-section' of the price-visitor relationship. In terms of Figure 5.1, it entailed looking at price and visitor information for a specific period across all the data cards.

Clearly, DoE and National Trust sites vary greatly in terms of their size, range of facilities and the quality of the recreational experience offered to visitors. Moreover, there is the paradoxical situation that the sites with the highest prices tend to have the highest visitor numbers. Of course, this is easily explained by the superior facilities which are offered at the highest priced sites - these superior facilities attract larger numbers of visitors and are used to justify the higher prices. However, because of the great difficulties in measuring the size and quality of facilities, it is difficult to standardise sites by including explicit 'attractiveness' variables. Cross-sectional analysis enables us to solve this problem by looking at the correlation between the change in the admission price at each site during the particular time period and the change in the number of visits to that site. This automatically eliminates the influence of location, size and quality of facilities upon the analysis of demand.

Longitudinal analysis

The longitudinal analysis involved comparing changes in the average number of visitors between two periods (each comprising a number of years) with changes in the average admission prices between the two periods. This allowed us to increase the number of factors for which we had standardised, especially variations in weather conditions. It also allowed us to encapsulate the longer-term effects of price changes, such as the 'rebound' of admissions in the year following a major price increase, and allowed us to derive estimates of price elasticity which were not subject to the volatility of short-term factors.

There are, however, two possible qualifications to the results of such longitudinal analysis. Firstly, they may gloss over secular trends. Secondly, as with cross-sectional analysis, if above average increases in the quality of facilities or in promotional activities were associated with above average increases in admission prices over the period analysed, then values for price elasticity are likely to be underestimates.

Time series analysis

The time series analysis involved comparing changes in the number of visits and admission prices at each site over a number of years. In terms of Figure 5.1 it entailed analysis of the price and visitor information on each separate card. This analysis allowed the effect of variations in admission prices and weather conditions on visitor numbers to be estimated for each individual site.

Time series analysis has a number of advantages over cross-sectional and longitudinal analysis. Firstly, it allowed us to identify the effects of variables which had similar values for all sites, such as increases in petrol prices and the retail prices index and which therefore could not be incorporated in a cross-sectional approach. Secondly, it allowed us to explore the possibility of a time-trend in visits to a site during all or part of the study period. Thirdly, it allowed a comparison of elasticity values for individual properties. Finally, it allowed us to investigate much more satisfactorily the influence of weather on visits, since we were able to use monthly rather than annual weather data.

The time series analyses which were undertaken explored how one site's visits over time were related to its own admission price levels and a range of factors which were likely to influence countryside recreational trip making in its catchment area - such as weather, incomes, unemployment, petrol costs, etc. However, it was not possible to include the effects of price changes at competitive sites. For this reason it was expected that the estimates of price elasticity derived from the time series analysis would tend to be underestimates (see Appendix A).

In the case of National Trust sites, however, this tendency was offset by the opportunity which National Trust visitors have to become members of the Trust and thereby gain 'free' admission to sites. Price increases at National Trust sites were expected to increase the extent to which this occurred, so that the estimates of price elasticity would make the National Trust sites appear more prone to losing visitors as a result of price increases than was really the case. Fortunately, the cross-sectional analysis of the National Trust sites was not prone to this drawback. Nevertheless, some separate analyses of the time series data for visits by National Trust members were carried out to enable us to correct for the possibility of such bias.

In conclusion, time series analysis was seen as a very powerful complement to cross-sectional analysis. However, the elasticity values derived for particular

DoE sites were likely to be underestimates; in the case of National Trust sites, two offsetting sources of bias occurred and it was not possible to say, a priori, which was likely to predominate.

Summary and conclusions

None of the forms of statistical analysis outlined above can be regarded as being entirely foolproof, or be expected to give results which can be accepted without careful interpretation. Nevertheless, given the complexity of the factors which influence demand for countryside recreation, only carefully conducted statistical analysis can hope to disentangle the effects of the major variables such as price, weather, etc. Each of these approaches is able to throw light on different aspects of the relationship between price changes and changes in the number of visits; together it is believed they provide a picture which is sufficiently accurate to give reliable guidance for policy making and site management decisions. In the following chapters we therefore summarise the results of these three approaches to estimating the responsiveness of demand to changes in admission prices at DoE and National Trust sites.

6 Cross-sectional analysis

Introduction

This chapter describes the results of a cross-sectional analysis of the relationship between changes in admission prices and changes in the number of visits to DoE and National Trust properties. It addresses four key questions:

(i) When some sites increase their prices more than others, do they generally experience a less favourable trend in visits than other sites?

(ii) If so, how much difference does it make to visits if a site increases its prices by 10% more than other sites?

(iii) Does this vary from year to year?

(iv) What effect does location, type of attractions or facilities and weather have on price elasticity?

Method of cross-sectional analysis

Cross-sectional analysis involves comparing admission prices and the number of visits between specific periods across a range of sites in order to obtain a 'cross-section' of the price-visitor relationship. As explained in Chapter 5, the method used in this study was to examine the change in admission prices at each site between two years and to correlate this with the change in the number of visits to that site. This automatically eliminated the influence of size and quality of facilities upon the analysis of demand - as long as we can make the assumption that these variables remain constant for each site during the period examined. While this assumption seems fair for most sites over a relatively short time period, it is possible for some biases to creep into the results (see Appendix A). In particular, if above average increases in price are associated with sites which increase or improve their facilities to an above average degree, or undertake large increases in their marketing and promotion, then the effect of price increases on admissions will tend to be underestimated.

In the first instance, simple regressions of year-on-year changes in the number of visits against changes in admission prices at each site were obtained. In order to isolate the possible distortions introduced by sites at which prices remained unchanged, sites which did not change their price in a particular year were excluded. All analyses were then repeated, regressing change in the number of visits to a site in a particular year against the change in admission prices in the previous year in order to identify any time lags in visitor reaction.

Further analyses were then carried out regressing changes in the number of visits against changes in weather as well as admission prices. The weather variables (indices for rainfall and sunshine in each year) were derived from the published and unpublished data covering the Meteorological Office's standard weather regions. Since these regions are fairly extensive, the indices are likely to reflect weather conditions both at the sites themselves and at the origins of most of the recreational trips made to them.

In addition to weather variables, these analyses also took account of the influence of the property type (i.e. whether it was a house, park, garden, castle, abbey, archaeological site, etc.) and the site's location relative to major population centres, holiday areas and National Parks. This was done by the inclusion of 'dummy' variables which described the characteristics of each site and which were allocated coefficients in the regression analysis which indicated the extent to which these characteristics tended to be associated with higher or lower levels of visits in the particular year under study. In this way year to year changes in the preferences of visitors for particular types or locations of site could be highlighted.

Measuring change in visitor numbers and price levels

Three different measures of change in admission prices and in the number of paying visitors were used in the analyses - percentage change, absolute change and logged change.

Percentage change

Percentage changes in the number of visitors between pairs of years were regressed against percentage changes in admission prices in the corresponding period. The resulting coefficient (the 'B' value in the tables which appear later in this chapter) can be interpreted as a crude elasticity value. This measure of change tends, however, to give undue weight to extreme fluctuations, especially in the case of sites with low prices. Results from this method of measuring change may therefore understate the true value of elasticity when the data contain a wide dispersion of percentage changes in price. Results calculated for separate categories of sites are therefore likely to be more reliable than results calculated for all sites together.

Absolute change

Absolute changes in the number of visitors were regressed against absolute changes in price and other relevant variables. This implies a linear demand function. Price elasticity changes continuously along such a demand function and can be calculated from the expression:

$$\text{price elasticity of demand} = \frac{P}{V} \cdot \frac{dV}{dP}$$

where P is the admission price, V is the number of visitors and dV/dP the rate of change of visits with respect to admission price, estimated by the coefficient of price in the regression equation (the 'B' value). With this demand function it is expected that for each site the price elasticity will be low at low prices and high at high prices. Following convention, the elasticity estimates quoted in this chapter apply only to the average values of visitors and admission price; elasticity values for other price levels should be calculated individually.

Logged change

The log of an index of changes in the number of visitors was regressed against the log of an index of changes in admission price and other relevant variables. This assumes a demand function in which the influences of all the independent variables are multiplied together rather than added together to estimate their overall effect on visitor demand. In this equation the value of the coefficient of price (the 'B' value) is a direct estimate of the price elasticity of demand. This function gives low weight to extreme values and it assumes constant elasticity at all prices. If different categories of sites turn out to have different constant terms and elasticity values, this is evidence that results obtained from the aggregation of sites (the 'all sites' analysis reported later) are not meaningful.

Price levels and changes

The years in which a significant number of price changes occurred at DoE sites were 1973, 1976, 1978 and 1980, as noted in Chapter 2. Cross-sectional analysis was therefore applied to changes in the numbers of paying visitors in each of these years and to changes in the year immediately following each major price rise, to test for lagged effects. It should be noted that the dramatic percentage increases in prices for many DoE sites in 1976 and for a smaller number of DoE sites in 1980 are likely to make the percentage change regression functions less reliable for these years.

Prices at National Trust sites were increased by varying amounts for a substantial number of sites in virtually every year from 1970 onwards, so that cross-sectional analyses can be carried out for each year. In some years, such as 1971, however, only a relatively small number of sites changed their admission prices. Generally, increases were smaller in percentage terms than at comparable DoE sites and, with the exception of 1970 and 1976, increases in admission prices amounting to more than 50% occurred at only a small minority of sites in each year. Even in 1970 and 1976 the sites showing such large percentage increases comprised less than 40% of the total number of sites analysed. Thus, while the percentage change regression functions in these two years are likely to provide less reliable estimates of elasticity than in other years, they are likely to be more reliable than for DoE sites.

Estimates of the price-visitor relationship

This section summarises the results of our analysis of the relationship between year-on-year changes in admission prices and changes in the number of paying visitors to sites. The tabular presentation of results is highly selective. More detailed statements of the statistical results can be found in Bovaird and Tricker (1982).

Department of Environment sites

For each year in which prices were increased, we find the expected negative relationship between changes in the number of visitors and changes in admission prices. Thus, as admission prices rise, the number of visitors to sites tends to fall. In general, however, a significant price effect was only identified for the price increases in 1976 and 1978, with the most significant relationship being found in 1976 - a year in which admission prices were doubled at the majority of sites. The price increases in 1973 and 1980, on the other hand do not appear to have had a statistically significant effect on changes in the number of visitors to sites.

The regression functions which related absolute changes in the number of visitors to absolute changes in admission prices consistently yielded more significant correlations than the percentage change or logged change functions (Tables 6.1, 6.4 and 6.7). This suggests that, within the range of real admission prices charged at DoE sites during this period, the demand curves were essentially linear for each group of sites. The slope of these demand curves tended to be lower for the smaller sites - this indicates that each size band should be considered on its own and that the results obtained by analysing all sites together are unreliable.

National Trust sites

For each year from 1970 to 1980, significant relationships between changes in the number of visitors and price changes were identified by at least one of the three functional forms adopted in the analysis (Tables 6.2, 6.5 and 6.8). The logged relationship between changes in the number of visitors and admission price changes was generally the most successful, giving significant results for more years and for more sites in different size and price bands than the other functional forms (Table 6.8). Anomalous figures were, however, produced for 1980 by the logged function.

Values of price elasticity

The percentage change function

In the case of DoE sites the values of price elasticity which emerged as significant from the percentage change regression function ranged from -0.08 for all sites with price changes in 1976 to -0.19 in 1978 for sites with relatively higher visitor numbers (Table 6.1). Whilst there appears to have been some increase in elasticity between 1976 and 1978, the percentage change regression did not identify a significant price relationship for 1980.

In the case of the National Trust sites, elasticity values estimated from the percentage change function ranged from -0.32 to -0.35 for higher priced sites and from -0.35 to -0.44 for larger sized sites (Table 6.2). This suggests that larger, high priced sites may have been the most price sensitive during this period.

There is strong evidence of a lagged effect of price changes on visitor numbers in the case of DoE sites. As shown in Table 6.3, the price changes of

Table 6.1

Relationship between % change in admission price and % change in paying visitors at DoE sites

(Excluding sites at which price remained unchanged)

R Squared

	All Sites	25+	10-25 (000 Paying Visitors)	10	Higher Priced	Lower Priced
1973	0.00 (42)	0.00 (30)	0.02 (8)	—	0.01 (41)	—
1976	0.07* (104)	0.08 (38)	0.04 (36)	0.06 (43)	0.21** (37)	0.05 (79)
1978	0.07 (40)	0.17* (26)	0.00 (10)	—	0.13* (29)	0.15 (11)
1980	0.03 (36)	0.07 (26)	—	—	0.01 (28)	—

B Values

1973	-0.02	-0.02	0.06	—	0.03	—
1976	-0.08	-0.11	-0.06	-0.09	-0.13	-0.08
1978	-0.21	-0.19	-0.06	—	-0.17	-0.91
1980	-0.09	-0.17	—	—	-0.10	—

** Significant correlation at 99% level

* Significant correlation at 95% level

Table 6.2

Relationship between % change in admission price and % change in paying visitors at National Trust sites

(Excluding sites at which price remained unchanged)

R Squared

	All Sites	25+	10-25 (000 Paying Visitors)	10	Higher Priced	Lower Priced
1970	0.03 (68)	0.04 (28)	0.10 (24)	0.01 (42)	0.10 (34)	0.00 (60)
1971	0.15 (17)	0.14 (8)	–	–	0.00 (9)	0.38* (10)
1972	0.01 (28)	0.08 (14)	0.15 (11)	0.06 (14)	0.02 (15)	0.02 (24)
1973	0.07 (45)	0.00 (19)	0.14 (17)	0.19* (18)	0.07 (22)	0.06 (32)
1974	0.05 (46)	0.08 (19)	0.04 (17)	0.11 (18)	0.03 (29)	0.10 (25)
1975	0.04 (47)	0.10 (27)	0.14 (11)	0.13 (19)	0.04 (25)	0.12 (32)
1976	0.00 (88)	0.02 (42)	0.13 (28)	0.02 (50)	0.24** (41)	0.00 (79)
1977						
1978	0.12** (57)	0.33** (30)	0.16 (13)	0.00 (29)	0.02 (22)	0.00 (50)
1979	0.03 (61)	0.12 (27)	0.00 (19)	0.01 (41)	0.04 (30)	0.00 (57)
1980	0.01 (87)	0.17** (41)	0.04 (25)	0.01 (49)	0.12* (42)	0.00 (73)

B Values

1970	0.02	0.07	0.63	−0.07	0.69	0.03
1971	0.24	−0.41	—	—	0.06	0.42
1972	−0.05	0.12	−0.29	0.27	−0.23	0.14
1973	−0.16	0.03	−0.23	−0.34	−0.21	−0.14
1974	−0.31	−0.42	−0.32	−0.81	−0.15	−0.74
1975	−0.15	−0.18	−0.51	−0.48	−0.24	−0.37
1976	−0.05	0.09	−0.24	−0.18	−0.35	−0.07
1977						
1978	−0.41	−0.44	−0.47	−0.59	−0.80	−0.49
1979	−0.15	−0.26	−0.04	0.13	0.14	−0.04
1980	−0.10	−0.35	0.30	−0.18	−0.32	−0.03

Table 6.3

Relationship between % change in admission price and % change in paying visitors in subsequent years at DoE sites

(Excluding sites at which price remained unchanged)

R Squared

	All Sites	25+	10-25 (000 Paying Visitors)	10	Higher Priced	Lower Priced
1973	0.19** (42)	0.16* (30)	0.52* (8)	—	0.19** (41)	—
1976	0.02 (108)	0.01 (40)	0.03 (30)	0.02 (39)	0.02 (37)	—
1978	0.04 (40)	0.18* (26)	0.34 (10)	—	0.15* (29)	0.03 (11)

B Values

	All Sites	25+	10-25	10	Higher Priced	Lower Priced
1973	<u>-0.12</u>	<u>-0.13</u>	<u>-0.21</u>	—	<u>-0.14</u>	—
1976	-0.05	0.06	-0.06	-0.05	0.00	—
1978	-0.15	<u>-0.24</u>	0.70	—	<u>-0.24</u>	0.32

both 1973 and 1978 were strongly correlated with the decreases in the number of visitors in the following year. Thus, the effects of the price rises lasted over two years. Their effects seem to have been mainly experienced at the larger and higher priced sites. No such relationships were found for National Trust sites, which suggests that this effect may be due to the DoE's practice of introducing large price increases at irregular intervals.

The absolute change function

The values of price elasticity for DoE sites in 1976 estimated from the absolute change regression function can be regarded as more reliable than those estimated by the percentage change functions; these ranged from around -0.35 to -0.40 for sites with relatively high numbers of visitors and prices to around -0.23 to -0.25 for sites with lower visitor numbers (Table 6.4). In 1978 the price elasticities estimated from the absolute change function ranged from around -0.16 to -0.23. There is thus strong evidence that elasticity was lower in 1978 than in 1976, in contrast to the results obtained from the percentage and logged change functions.

Since the dispersion of annual percentage changes in admission prices to National Trust sites was generally lower than in the case of DoE sites, the elasticity estimates derived from the absolute change function were expected to be similar to those derived from the percentage change function. Whilst this was generally the case, significant relationships were found over a wider range of site categories (Table 6.5). Moreoever, the elasticities estimated from this analysis were generally slightly higher than those estimated from the percentage change function.

Again, there is strong evidence of a lagged effect of price changes on visitor numbers to DoE sites. This shows up more clearly in the absolute change functions than in others (Table 6.6). Thus, for sites which raised their prices in 1973, a further significant fall in the number of visitors occurred in 1974. However, in 1977 those sites which had increased their prices most in 1976 showed a relative recovery in the number of paying visitors in the subsequent year. The 1978 price increases once again appear to have reduced the number of paying visitors in 1979. These effects appeared to be largely confined to those sites with relatively high numbers of visitors and relatively higher prices - the sites which showed the greatest visitor responses to price increases in 1976 and 1978. The behaviour of visitors after the very high price rises of 1976 may be a further indication of the extent to which very large price increases can have a very damaging short-run effect.

Logged change function

Given the success of the absolute change formulation in yielding significant equations, estimates derived for DoE sites from the logged function must be regarded with caution; in particular its assumption of constant elasticity at all price levels seems to be questioned by the changing elasticities at different prices which are implied by the absolute change function. Nevertheless, the logged function supplies a useful corrective to the likely underestimate of price elasticity emerging from the percentage change function. The logged function estimates ranged from -0.21 in 1976 for all sites experiencing a price change, to around -0.30 in 1976 and 1978 at sites with relatively higher prices and higher

Table 6.4

Relationship between absolute change in admission price and change in number of paying visitors at DoE sites

(Excluding sites at which price remained unchanged)

R Squared

	All Sites	25+	10-25 (000 Paying Visitors)	10	Higher Priced	Lower Priced
1973	0.14** (41)	0.19* (32)	—	—	0.14* (41)	—
1976	0.35** (106)	0.32** (40)	0.10 (36)	0.13* (39)	0.31** (40)	0.02 (77)
1978	0.66** (39)	0.67** (26)	0.04 (10)	—	0.68** (29)	—
1980	0.05 (35)	0.05 (26)	—	—	0.06 (28)	—

B Values

	All Sites	25+	10-25	10	Higher Priced	Lower Priced
1973	-849	-1035	—	—	-848	—
1976	-1317	-1420	-204	-173	-1385	-215
1978	-898	-921	-238	—	-921	—
1980	-400	-373	—	—	-419	—

Table 6.5

Relationship between absolute change in admission price and change in number of paying visitors at National Trust sites

(Excluding sites at which price remained unchanged)

R Squared

	All Sites	25+	10-25 (000 Paying Visitors)	10	Higher Priced	Lower Priced
1970	0.00 (70)	0.02 (28)	0.00 (24)	0.13* (42)	0.00 (34)	0.02 (60)
1971	0.02 (17)	0.08 (8)	—	0.05 (7)	—	0.08 (10)
1972	0.01 (30)	0.01 (14)	—	0.00 (14)	0.06 (15)	0.05 (24)
1973	0.04 (45)	0.01 (19)	0.22 (17)	0.06 (18)	0.09 (22)	0.03 (32)
1974	0.03 (46)	0.06 (19)	—	0.02 (18)	0.02 (22)	0.06 (25)
1975	0.06 (47)	0.02 (27)	0.13 (17)	0.26 (19)	0.07 (25)	0.09 (32)
1976	0.04 (90)	0.04 (42)	0.02 (28)	0.09 (50)	0.25** (41)	0.02 (79)
1977						
1978	0.02 (57)	0.15* (30)	0.24 (13)	0.00 (29)	0.08 (22)	0.01 (50)
1979	0.02 (61)	0.17* (27)	0.00 (19)	0.01 (41)	0.02 (30)	0.05 (57)
1980	0.16** (87)	0.18** (41)	0.31** (25)	0.10* (49)	0.17** (40)	0.18** (75)

B Values

1970	−79	−270	123	−103	82	−116
1971	−245	−914	—	−99	—	−238
1972	304	487	—	19	−947	543
1973	−350	−300	−405	−116	−296	−435
1974	−278	−430	—	−42	−199	−446
1975	−1	−1	−1	−7	−1	−3
1976	−178	−222	−79	−53	−366	122
1977						
1978	−257	−784	396	26	−436	−172
1979	−87	−376	23	−17	71	−156
1980	−259	−384	−178	−52	−229	−393

Table 6.6

Relationship between absolute change in admission price and change in number of paying visitors in subsequent years at DoE sites

(Excluding sites at which price remained unchanged)

R Squared

	All Sites	25+	10-25 (000 Paying Visitors)	10	Higher Priced	Lower Priced
1973	0.44** (41)	0.45** (32)	—	—	0.44** (41)	—
1976	0.36** (106)	0.39** (40)	0.00 (30)	0.02 (39)	0.39** (39)	0.02
1978	0.78** (39)	0.77** (26)	0.00 (10)	—	0.76** (29)	—

B Values

1973	-8740	-9394	—	—	-8740	—
1976	3057	3676	-27	-56	3708	-244
1978	-1321	-1338	62		-1325	—

visitor numbers (Table 6.7). Again, there is an indication that elasticity may have been higher in 1978 than 1976. Significant equations were not generally found for sites with relatively lower visitor numbers and lower prices.

Logged function elasticity values for National Trust sites with relatively higher prices and higher visitor numbers ranged from around -0.30 to around -0.60. With the exception of 1971, the elasticities for medium sized sites fell within the same range. Few significant relationships between changes in admission prices and changes in numbers of visits were found for smaller and lower priced sites, (Table 6.8).

The influence of other variables on the price-visitor relationship

For all sites in the DoE and National Trust data sets, including those which did not change their price in the particular year studied, the influence of other variables was analysed. The main additional variables were weather indices (sunshine levels, number of rain days in the year), locational variables (urban, urban fringe within 10 miles of a major urban area, urban influenced between 10 and 25 miles of a major urban area, within a holiday area, within a national park) and property type.

The overall level of explanation of percentage changes in the number of paying visitors was increased substantially when additional variables designed to take account of variations in location in relation to major urban centres, holiday areas and national parks, different property types and regional variations in weather were introduced in to the analysis. In the case of DoE sites, however, price did not make a significant contribution to the explanation of variations in percentage changes in visitor numbers in any year other than 1976 (Table 6.9). The major significant influences on changes in visitor numbers identified by this analysis were indices of changes in the amount of sunshine between regions and the group of 'dummy' variables designed to indicate location of sites in relation to major urban centres. In 1976, when price did enter the equation as a significant variable, the 'B' value suggested a very similar elasticity to that identified in the simple bivariate analysis (Table 6.9 compared with Table 6.1).

In the case of National Trust sites the level of explanation was generally enhanced when indices of variations in weather conditions and property type indices were introduced. 'Dummy' variables indicating location in holiday areas or within national parks appeared as particularly significant additional variables in the equations. Generally, the significance of admission price was enhanced as a result, but the 'B' values, and hence the estimated elasticity values, remained very similar to those estimated by the simple bivariate analysis. When the data was disaggregated by size and price, however, reactions to price increases in 1976 and 1977 implied slightly higher elasticities for sites in the higher price ranges with a particularly high value of -0.82 in 1977. (Table 6.10(c)).

Very similar values were obtained when the logged function was applied to the wider set of variables to estimate changes in the number of visits to National Trust sites (Table 6.11). Elasticity values estimated from this formulation range from around -0.16 to -0.43 for all sites considered together; -0.50 to-0.86 for higher priced sites; -0.20 to -0.68 for sites with higher visitor numbers, and somewhat higher values of -0.40 to -0.90 for sites within the medium size range.

Table 6.7

Relationship between log change in admission price and log change in number of paying visitors at DoE sites

(Excluding sites at which price remained unchanged)

R Squared

	All Sites	25+	10-25 (000 Paying Visitors)	10	Higher Priced	Lower Priced
1973	0.01 (41)	0.00 (32)	—	—	0.01 (41)	—
1976	0.08** (93)	0.11* (40)	0.03 (36)	0.06 (43)	0.17** (40)	0.04 (79)
1978	0.08 (37)	0.18* (26)	0.00 (10)	—	0.15* (29)	0.13 (11)
1980	0.03 (33)	0.08 (26)	0.18 (7)	—	0.01	0.03

B Values

	All Sites	25+	10-25	10	Higher Priced	Lower Priced
1973	-0.05	-0.03	—	—	-0.05	—
1976	-0.21	-0.28	-0.13	-0.27	-0.29	-0.23
1978	-0.40	-0.32	-0.07	—	-0.29	-1.40
1980	-0.16	-0.30	-0.23	—	-0.17	-0.29

Table 6.8

Relationship between log change in admission price and log change in number of paying visitors at National Trust sites

(Excluding sites at which price remained unchanged)

R Squared

	All Sites	25+	10-25 (000 Paying Visitors)	10	Higher Priced	Lower Priced
1970	—	0.00 (42)	0.01 (28)	0.03 (42)	0.03 (37)	0.01 (84)
1971	0.03 (92)	0.10* (43)	0.18* (27)	—	0.15* (38)	0.00 (84)
1972	0.06* (96)	0.06 (45)	0.05 (29)	0.00 (16)	0.02 (40)	0.01 (87)
1973	0.07** (97)	0.05 (45)	0.22** (29)	0.17 (19)	0.11* (41)	0.01 (88)
1974	0.08** (99)	0.05 (46)	0.17* (30)	0.14 (18)	0.10 (41)	0.00 (90)
1975	0.09** (98)	0.15** (45)	0.24** (30)	0.15 (19)	0.10* (41)	0.05* (88)
1976	0.03 (98)	0.01 (45)	0.10 (30)	0.04 (50)	0.25** (41)	0.01 (88)
1977				0.20 (29)		
1978	0.18** (93)	0.43** (44)	0.19* (28)	0.02 (29)	0.01 (40)	0.02 (85)
1979	0.04 (88)	0.29 ** (44)	0.00 (26)	0.00 (41)	—	0.02 (82)
1980	0.34 ** (91)	0.58** (44)	—	0.02 (49)	0.16* (40)	0.33** (87)

B Values

1970	—	0.03	0.17	−0.19	0.25	−0.06
1971	−0.22	−0.48	−1.38	—	−0.57	0.10
1972	−0.25	−0.21	−0.34	−0.05	−0.17	−0.13
1973	−0.22	−0.16	−0.38	−0.37	−0.30	−0.16
1974	−0.35	−0.25	−0.51	−0.89	−0.29	−0.09
1975	−0.27	−0.27	−0.61	−0.66	−0.33	−0.24
1976	−0.17	−0.07	−0.31	−0.33	−0.57	−0.14
1977						
1978	−0.48	−0.61	−0.51	0.37	−0.18	−0.27
1979	−0.29	−0.56	0.11	0.07	—	−0.22
1980	2.17	3.24	—	−0.28	−0.52	2.20

This analysis in particular, highlights the tendency for elasticity values to increase towards the end of the study period and to be a little higher when the influence of other variables is allowed for.

The influence of other variables on visitor numbers

The influence of weather

The interpretation of the influence of the selected weather variables on visitor numbers is unclear. While, in general, higher amounts of sunshine and lower rainfall both tend to be associated with increases in visitor numbers, the relationship is not consistent nor markedly strong. Not only do the rain and sunshine variables appear in many regressions to have the opposite sign to that expected, but they also do not figure at all in many regressions. Given the highly 'peaked' nature of the distribution of visits to most sites, it may be that there is a need to use more precise weather data, which concentrates on the weather in the peak three months of each year only. Alternatively, as suggested in Appendix A, separate analyses for each region might ensure that the weather region data were not acting purely as regional proxies rather than as weather variables.

The influence of petrol prices

The location variables allow us to test for the possible influence of the increase in real petrol prices in 1974-75 and 1979-80. In 1974 the larger National Trust sites in urban areas and smaller National Trust sites in and around urban areas had favourable visitor trends. (Tables 6.10(a), (b) and (c)). In 1975 the direct advantage of urban or urban influenced location does not show up again (since this is a comparison of 1975 with 1974 patterns), but the strong trends against larger sites in national parks may indicate that more remote sites were still suffering some of the effects of the petrol price rises (Tables 6.10(a) and 6.11). In 1979 urban fringe and urban influenced sites in fact tended to do rather badly, except for the larger sites (Tables 6.10(a) and 6.11), in spite of the petrol price rise and in 1980 there were contrasting experiences, with urban influenced DoE sites doing well (especially the larger, higher priced sites), but National Trust urban sites doing badly (especially the larger sites and the medium priced sites). These results reinforce the argument put forward in Chapter 3 that there is not a simple causal link between higher petrol prices and decreases in the number of countryside recreation trips.

The influence of parkland amenities

Sites with parkland amenities were not strongly associated with any of the other property type variables or location variables. Their influence on the equations in Tables 6.10 and 6.11, therefore, should reflect only changing demands for parkland amenities. These equations show that the influence of parkland amenities on visitor numbers tended to vary quite sharply from year to year. In some years, parkland amenities were associated with high increases in the number of visitors (for example in 1978 for smaller, cheaper sites) but in other years such amenities were associated with decreases (for example in 1979 for larger sites) and in most years the presence or absence of such facilities does

Table 6.9

Relationship between % change in full rate paying visitors and site characteristics in years of main price changes at DoE sites

	Conceptual Variables	Price	Weather Indices		Locational Variables					Type		Statistics	
	Specific Measures / Year	Adult Admission Price	Sunshine Level	Rain Days	Urban	Urban Fringe <10 Miles	Urban Influence >10<25 Miles	Holiday Area	National Park	Park	Gardens	R^2	N
Sites with more than 25,000 paying visitors in 1975	1973		0.94**		−7.49			11.92**				0.28	39
	1976	−0.11**	−0.48		−10.86**							0.23	39
	1978								10.41*			0.10	41
	1980	−0.11		−0.69*			21.13**					0.44	26
Sites with fewer than 10,000 paying visitors in 1975	1973		1.47**			13.46*						0.30	44
	1976	0.08*	0.59*		16.91*	−17.66**	−17.47**	10.18*				0.38	44
	1978		−1.78**					11.08*				0.26	32
	1980	—	—	—	—	—	—	—	—	—	—	—	—

Table 6.10

Relationship between % change in full rate paying visitors and site characteristics at National Trust sites

(a) Sites with more than 25,000 visitors in 1975

Conceptual Variables	Price	Weather Indices		Locational Variables					Type		Statistics	
Specific Measures / Year	Adult Admission Price	Sunshine Level	Rain Days	Urban	Urban Fringe <10 Miles	Urban Influence >10<25 Miles	Holiday Area	National Park	Park	Gardens	R^2	N
1969		0.17		48.84**			-17.68**			-12.45	0.59	34
1970			-0.32								0.25	38
1971	-0.55**						5.79					
1972	-0.24**	-0.94		-20.86**		-4.59		15.05**	6.85*	-15.30**	0.69	32
1973		0.95*	0.48								0.46	37
1974				66.94**			6.40				0.73	37
1975	-0.23**	0.66	-0.80**					-18.86**	-0.43**		0.63	37
1976			0.34				24.52**	-24.74**			0.46	39
1977		-0.63									0.27	41
1978	-0.51**			10.47							0.65	40
1979	-0.47**	-0.58		-6.93	8.28	7.96**	-11.46**		-10.52**	5.52	0.73	34
1980				-30.00*						9.28	0.43	40

Table 6.10

Relationship between % change in full rate paying visitors and site characteristics at National Trust sites

(b) Sites with less than 5,000 visitors

Conceptual Variables	Price	Weather Indices		Locational Variables					Type		Statistics	
Specific Measures / Year	Adult Admission Price	Sunshine Level	Rain Days	Urban	Urban Fringe <10 Miles	Urban Influence >10 <25 Miles	Holiday Area	National Park	Park	Gardens	R^2	N
1969		0.62	−1.48**								0.50	22
1970			−1.07								0.31	23
1971							29.10				0.17	23
1972									−16.33		0.14	23
1973		−2.09									0.25	23
1974					75.45**					16.94	0.66	22
1975	0.43						−43.56**				0.56	25
1976						−28.90					0.33	26
1977	−0.23		−1.02*								0.44	25
1978						63.73*	−20.09		83.68**		0.62	24
1979						−18.02					0.27	26
1980		−8.16**	−1.45								0.58	25

Table 6.10

Relationship between % change in full rate paying bisitors and site characteristics at National Trust sites

(c) Sites with an admission charge of more than 30 pence in 1975

Conceptual Variables	**Price**	**Weather Indices**		**Locational Variables**					**Type**		**Statistics**	
Specific Measures / Year	Adult Admission Price	Sunshine Level	Rain Days	Urban	Urban Fringe <10 Miles	Urban Influence >10<25 Miles	Holiday Area	National Park	Park	Gardens	R^2	N
1969				65.43**	5.2		-15.28**	20.61*			0.61	30
1970			-0.63	225.03**			14.62**				0.94	31
1971	-0.44**		-2.90**	-20.83				-41.95**			0.55	30
1972	0.27							30.36**			0.47	32
1973			0.44								0.26	33
1974	-0.28**					- 8.03	12.42**		-10.55**		0.58	30
1975		1.38*		-17.59			-19.26**				0.53	36
1976	-0.43**		-0.46**	17.12		-14.39**			-7.47**		0.74	34
1977	-0.82**			27.33**				23.29**		7.4	0.63	35
1978				34.76							0.30	38
1979			0.58								0.22	38
1980	-0.30*							-13.94			0.42	37

Table 6.11

Influences on the annual change in the number of paying visitors (log function) at National Trust sites with more than 25,000 visitors in 1975

Conceptual Variables	Price	Weather Indices		Locational Variables					Type		Statistics	
Specific Measures / Year	Adult Admission Price	Sunshine Level	Rain Days	Urban	Urban Fringe <10 Miles	Urban Influence >10<25 Miles	Holiday Area	National Park	Park	Gardens	R^2	N
1970			−0.32*					0.07			0.11	40
1971	−0.55**		−0.28								0.16	40
1972	−0.29**			−0.20**		−0.07		0.11*	0.05	−0.14**	0.47	40
1973		0.89*	0.41*	−0.14							0.26	40
1974	−0.21*			0.50**	−0.09						0.53	40
1975	−0.30**	−0.62	−0.55*					−0.18**	−0.09**		0.32	45
1976							0.18**	−0.19		−0.07	0.17	45
1977	−0.40**					−0.03	0.09*				0.27	45
1978	−0.68**	−0.32									0.36	43
1979	−0.60**				0.11*		−0.06*		−0.10**	0.07*	0.52	43
1980	3.01**	17.88**	6.12*	−0.64							0.70	43

Table 6.12

Influences on the annual change in the number of paying visitors at National Trust sites with parks

Conceptual Variables	Price	Weather Indices		Locational Variables					Statistics	
Specific Measures / Year	Adult Admission Price	Sunshine Level	Rain Days	Urban	Urban Fringe <10 Miles	Urban Influence >10<25 Miles	Holiday	National	R^2	N
1975				−0.26*	+0.11	−0.11			0.36	26
1976	−0.52**					0.09			0.28	27
1977	−0.56*						0.15**		0.46	27
1978	−0.36**			0.27**	−0.17**	0.08			0.60	26
1979	−0.24				0.16				0.35	26
1980	−0.40*						−0.18**		0.44	26

not appear as a significant influence on visitor numbers.

A separate question is whether sites with parkland amenities have a different value of price elasticity from the other types of sites included in our cross-sectional analysis. In order to test this possibility separate regressions for National Trust sites with parks were carried out, using the logged function which performed best for National Trust sites overall. The results show that price was a significant, or almost significant, influence on changes in the number of visits to National Trust sites with parks in every year from 1976 to 1980; the value of price elasticity ranged from -0.24 in 1979 to -0.56 in 1977 (Table 6.12). These estimates are consistent with, if perhaps a little lower than, the price elasticity values for all National Trust sites summarised above.

Summary and conclusions

The best estimate for price elasticity at DoE sites from the cross-sectional analysis is between -0.15 and -0.40 (from the absolute change regression functions). Price elasticity may well have decreased between 1976 and 1978 and changes in admission prices appear to have had even less influence on changes in the number of visitors in 1980.

The best estimates for price elasticity at National Trust sites is between -0.30 and -0.60 for sites with high prices or large or medium visitor numbers. It appears that higher priced sites may have had elasticities above -0.60 in 1978 but there is no indication that this continued to be true in 1979 and 1980. Visits to smaller and lower priced sites did not in general appear to be significantly influenced by changes in admission prices in this period.

7 Longitudinal analysis

Introduction

This chapter examines the data used in the cross-sectional analysis in a different and longer-term perspective. It addresses five key questions:

(i) When some sites increase their prices more than others over a period of years, are the effects on visits more significant than the year-on-year changes described in Chapter 6?

(ii) If so, what is the value of the longer-term price elasticity?

(iii) Has this varied over the decade studied?

(iv) What have been the longer-term changes in visitor numbers at sites in different locations and with different attractions?

(v) What has been the effect of admission price changes at National Trust sites on the proportion of visits by non-members?

Method of longitudinal analysis

From the results of the cross-sectional analysis summarised in Chapter 6, it was apparent that significant lagged responses to price increases occurred in some years during the study period. One way to incorporate these lags more satisfactorily into the analysis, and thus to obtain more accurate estimates of the price elasticity of demand, was to correlate changes in the number of visitors with changes in admission prices over longer time periods.

It was also apparent from the cross-sectional analysis that the influence of weather was not emerging as strongly as had been expected. The time series analysis described in Chapter 8 did however, confirm that variations in weather from month to month do have an important and significant effect on changes in the number of visitors to individual sites. It was therefore concluded that the annual indices of variations in weather conditions used in the cross-sectional analysis were probably too crude to estimate these effects accurately and as a result, indices of changes in weather between sub-periods were not included in this part of the analysis.

Ideally, therefore, the sub-periods for which averages are calculated should be long enough to contain within them not only all the lagged responses of visits to changes in admission prices but also a typical range of weather conditions. This is, however, unlikely to be true of shorter sub-periods comprising only two or three years. This qualification should be borne in mind when interpreting results from analyses based on these sub-periods. The groupings of time periods adopted for DoE sites are given in Figure 7.1.

First period	Second period	Table reference
1970/72	1973/75	Table 7.1
1973/75	1976/77	Table 7.2
1976/77	1978/79	Table 7.3
1978/79	1980 only	Table 7.4
1970/75	1976/80	Table 7.5
1970/72	1978/79	Tables 7.6 and 7.7
1973/75	1976/80	Table 7.8

Figure 7.1

Time periods used for comparisons in longitudinal analysis of the price-visitor relationship at DoE sites

In the first instance, analysis was carried out by grouping data around years of major price changes. Variations in admission prices and numbers of paying visitors between sub-periods were expressed as percentage changes, absolute changes and logged changes.

This grouping of data gave some interesting and useful results for DoE sites. The timing of increases at individual National Trust sites, however, varied appreciably, so there were no very clear groupings of years between which tests of price-visitor relationships could be carried out. The tests on grouped data which were carried out confirmed that, because of this variation, it was not possible to detect any significant relationships by this approach.

For similar reasons, grouping data for DoE sites around the years of 1978 and 1980 was not as successful in identifying a significant relationship as in earlier years since such short time periods did not allow the full lagged responses to appear, especially when further price increases occurred in subsequent years. An attempt was made to overcome this problem in two ways: firstly by comparing changes over much longer time spans, such as 1970-75 with 1976-79, in order to smooth out these lagged changes, and secondly by comparing the number of visits in the earlier years of the study period (1970-72) with those of later years (1978-79 for DoE sites and 1979-80 for National Trust sites). The latter approach had the advantage of maximising variations in the admission charges to sites, and therefore increased the possibility of detecting the full influence of price changes on admissions.

Finally, in recognition of the substantial growth in National Trust membership over this period and the increasing importance of members as a proportion of the total number of visitors to sites, a separate analysis of the relationship between this trend and increases in admission prices was undertaken.

The price-visitor relationship at DoE sites

Period 1970-75

For the three years before and after 1973, all functional forms indicated price to be a very significant determinant of changes in visitor numbers. Estimates of price elasticities were, however, much greater for medium-sized sites (range -0.30 to -0.51) than for the larger sites (range -0.19 to -0.29) (Table 7.1).

Period 1973-77

Comparing visits in 1976-77 with visits in the three years before, admission price was again picked out as one of the most significant variables for most site sizes under all functional forms. Price elasticities were in the range -0.09 to -0.11 using the percentage change demand function; and in the range -0.17 to -0.28 for the logged demand function. The evidence that a logged demand function appeared to work well for all sizes of site was consistent with the absolute change function giving non-significant price effects for large sites. In addition, the very high price rises in 1976 were expected to lead to an underestimate of price elasticity in the percentage change equations. It therefore appears likely that the logged demand functions were a more reliable estimator of the effects of the 1976 price increases. These indicated that price elasticity was similar for large and medium-sized sites (about -0.17 to -0.20) but probably rather larger for smaller sites (around -0.28) (Table 7.2).

Period 1976-80

Analysis of the effects of changes in admission prices on visits before and after 1978 was constrained by the small sample of medium and small sites. However, it was quite clear that the larger sites included in the sample had a relatively high price elasticity during this period. Using the percentage change function the estimate was in the range -0.22 to -0.33; under the absolute change function it was in the range -0.55 to -0.57; and under the logged demand function it ranged from -0.29 to -0.33 (Table 7.3). The problem here is how to interpret the especially high elasticity value calculated under the absolute change function. It appears likely that this was largely due to one site (Hampton Court) which increased its admission price by 50 pence. This site experienced a fall in visitors over the period 1978-79 of 97,000. No other site in the sample increased its admission price by more than 20 pence. Finally, no significant relationships between changes in admission prices and changes in the number of visitors were found in comparing 1978/79 with 1980 data (Table 7.4).

Table 7.1

Influences on the change in the number of full rate paying visitors in a group of years around 1973 (1970/2 - 1973/5) at DoE sites with more than 25,000 visitors in 1975

Conceptual Variables	Price	Locational Variables			Area Type	Building Type					Statistics	
Specific Measures / Equation Type	Adult Admission Price	Urban	Urban Fringe <10 miles	Urban Influence >10 <25 Miles	Holiday Area	Archaeological Site	Castle	Abbey	Priory	House	R^2	N
Percentage Change	−0.19**	26.0**	−13.9*								0.44	24
Absolute Change	−0.19**	72100**	−34200*			103100**	19600			61300*	0.81	24
Log of Changes	−0.29**	0.24**	−0.12*			0.12					0.52	24

Table 7.2

Influences on the change in the number of full rate paying visitors in a group of years around 1976 (1973/5 - 1976/7) at DoE sites with more than 25,000 visitors in 1975

Conceptual Variables	**Price**	**Locational Variables**			**Area Type**	**Building Type**					**Statistics**	
Specific Measures / Equation Type	Adult Admission Price	Urban	Urban Fringe <10 miles	Urban Influence >10 <25 Miles	Holiday Area	Archaeological Site	Castle	Abbey	Priory	House	R^2	N
Percentage Change	−0.09	26.1**							−16.1**		0.28	39
Absolute Change			44300*		−76300	−82600**	−53600**	−61000*	−72300**		0.38	39
Log of Changes	−0.20*	0.24**							−0.15**	0.13	0.31	39

Table 7.3

Influences on the change in the number of full rate paying visitors in a group of years around 1978 (1976/7 - 1978/9) at DoE sites with more than 25,000 visitors in 1975

Conceptual Variables	Price	Locational Variables			Area Type	Building Type					Statistics	
Specific Measures / Equation Type	Adult Admission Price	Urban	Urban Fringe <10 miles	Urban Influence >10<25 Miles	Holiday Area	Archaeological Site	Castle	Abbey	Priory	House	R^2	N
Percentage Change	−0.33**	10.6*				−12.1**	−12.7**		−8.7		0.52	27
Absolute change	−0.55**				34600*		−21700**		−12700	41100**	0.77	27
Log of Changes	−0.33**	0.10*						0.10*		0.12*	0.47	27

Table 7.4

Influences on the change in the number of full rate paying visitors in a group of years around 1980 (1978/9 - 1980) at DoE sites with more than 25,000 visitors in 1975

Conceptual Variables	**Price**	**Locational Variables**			**Area Type**	**Building Type**					**Statistics**	
Specific Measures / Equation Type	Adult Admission Price	Urban	Urban Fringe <10 miles	Urban Influence >10<25 Miles	Holiday Area	Archaeological Site	Castle	Abbey	Priory	House	R^2	N
Percentage Change	−0.14						16.3**	12.3			0.41	26
Absolute Change		No significant equation										
Log of Changes	−0.26						0.18**	0.14*				

Longer period comparisons 1970-80

Analysis of changes in admission prices and visits over longer time periods was also constrained to some extent by data availability. Thus, comparison of changes in visits and price levels between the 1970-75 and 1976-80 periods was only possible for 19 DoE sites. The elasticity values estimated for these ranged from -0.24 to -0.36. Clearly however, the effects of the 1980 price increases are not likely to be fully reflected in this period and it would appear more sensible to assume that the true elasticity value is likely to be nearer the top end of this range. Nevertheless, the high elasticity values estimated for larger sites (Table 7.5) are likely to be misleading and unreliable, given that only 14 sites were included.

Analysis of changes between the 1970-72 and 1978-79 periods suggested price elasticities in the range from -0.30 to -0.41. Those sites with relatively high numbers of visitors and higher prices, however, appear to have had rather lower elasticities over this period (Table 7.6 and 7.7). This contrasts with the estimates derived from a comparison of the 1976-77 and 1978-79 periods and probably indicates relatively low elasticities for the larger sites from 1970 up to 1977. This appears to be confirmed by the analysis of changes between the periods from 1973-75 to 1976-78 which yielded elasticity estimates from -0.11 to -0.17 with no definite pattern of higher elasticites for larger sites. Averages for 1973-75 compared with those for 1976-80 gave slightly higher price elasticites for sites with higher visitor numbers (Table 7.8). For both these periods the percentage change regressions, which yielded the lower estimates, are likely to underestimate the true values.

The price-visitor relationship at National Trust sites

As discussed earlier, regressions for relatively short groups of years did not identify significant price-visitor relationships at National Trust sites. Attention was therefore focussed on changes between rather longer periods. The periods chosen for comparison were 1970-75 with 1976-80, 1973-75 with 1976-78 and 1970-72 with 1978-80.

The only significant price effect in all these regressions was a weak <u>positive</u> price effect, using the absolute change function, for 1970/75-1976/80. In all other cases, admission price appears to have been an insignificant factor in explaining the variations of visitor numbers between the two sub-periods. As noted earlier, this low level of association between changes in admission prices and changes in the number of visits between relatively short sub-periods is probably due in part to variations in the timing of price increases at individual sites. As a result, the extent to which the full effects of lagged responses are incorporated in any given sub-period varies between sites. However, this explanation is less likely to be true for the longer sub-periods such as 1970-75 and 1976-80.

This apparent insensitivity of changes in the number of visits to increases in admission charges may be due in part to the effects of the promotional activities of the National Trust. This has included not only improvements to facilities at many of the individual sites which have subsequently raised their prices, but also a sustained campaign aimed at increasing the membership of the Trust. The effect of this large scale rise in membership is examined in the next section.

Table 7.5

Influences on the change in the number of full rate paying visitors between the 1970-75 period and the 1976-80 period at DoE sites with more than 25,000 visitors in 1975

Conceptual Variables	Price	Locational Variables			Area Type	Building Type					Statistics	
Specific Measures / Equation Type	Adult Admission Price	Urban	Urban Fringe <10 miles	Urban Influence >10 <25 Miles	Holiday Area	Archaeological Site	Castle	Abbey	Priory	House	R^2	N
Percentage Change	−0.62**	34.8**	−11.7*	24.0**				13.8*		21.5**	0.89	14
Absolute Change	−388470 **	24300**		24025**	13180*			9940		54513**	0.90	14
Log of Changes	−0.95**	0.38**	−0.12	0.28**				0.16		0.26*	0.89	14

Table 7.6

Influences on the change in the number of full rate paying visitors between the 1970/72 period and the 1978/79 period at DoE sites with more than 25,000 visitors in 1975

Conceptual Variables	**Price**	**Locational Variables**			**Area Type**	**Building Type**					**Statistics**		
Specific Measures / Equation Type	Adult Admission Price	Urban	Urban Fringe <10 miles	Urban Influence >10<20 Miles	Holiday Area	Arch-aeological Site	Castle	Abbey	Priory	House	Constant	R^2	N
Percentage Change	−0.20*	49.2**	−20.3*			16.1		28.4*			4.3	0.87	14
Absolute Change	−238590**	41000*					−38060**	−19240	−41580**		44180	0.93	14
Log of Change	−0.31*	0.56*					−0.19*				6.27	0.84	14

Table 7.7

Influences on the change in the number of full rate paying visitors between the 1970/72 period and the 1978/79 period at DoE sites with an admission charge of more than 30 pence in 1975

Conceptual Variables	Price	Locational Variables			Area Type		Building Type				Statistics		
Specific Measures / Equation Type	Adult Admission Price	Urban	Urban Fringe <10 miles	Urban Influence >10<20 Miles	Holiday Area	Arch-aeological Site	Castle	Abbey	Priory	House	Constant	R^2	N
Percentage Change	−0.21**	31.33**	−16.6		−9.63*		−17.93**				23.15	0.84	15
Absolute Change	−219657**						−35674**	−18032			42145	0.86	15
Log of Change	−0.29*	0.26*			−0.11*		−0.20**				6.19	0.77	15

Table 7.8

Influences on the change in the number of full rate paying visitors between the 1973/75 period and the 1976/80 period at DoE sites with more than 25,000 visitors in 1975

Conceptual Variables	Price	Locational Variables			Area Type	Building Type					Statistics		
Specific Measures / Equation Type	Adult Admission Price	Urban	Urban Fringe <10 miles	Urban Influence >10<20 Miles	Holiday Area	Arch-aeological Site	Castle	Abbey	Priory	House	Constant	R^2	N
Percentage Change	−0.16*	44.3**						8.6	−23.4**	16.1*	−7.2	0.59	26
Absolute Change	−162560**	−14365*								30980**	−4.360	0.47	26
Log of Change	−0.23*	−0.42**							−0.28**	0.14	5.6	0.63	26

Visits by National Trust members

The rise in National Trust membership has been a national rather than a regional or localised phenomenon. We would therefore not expect the increase in admission prices at individual sites to play such an important role in the decision to join as the cost of membership relative to admission prices in general. However, for individual sites, we would nevertheless expect that the relative level of admission charges would influence the ratio of members to paying visitors through the deterrent effect which high prices are likely to have on non-members. Thus, the proportion of paying visitors to members' visits would be expected to decrease especially fast for those sites raising their admission charges most. However, the low correlation reported earlier between changes in admission prices and changes in the number of paying visitors over the longer sub-periods, may also reflect differential growth in National Trust membership between regions.

Analyses of the relationship between changes in the number of visits by members and changes in admission prices between the 1970-75 and the 1976-80 period indicated that price was significant for the absolute change and logged change equations and implied an elasticity value of around +0.40 (Table 7.9). This indicates that sites with a 10% increase in admission charges relative to all other sites are likely to have a 4% rise in visits by members, relative to all other sites. This relationship may have arisen because the price increases at individual sites have a significant local effect in encouraging casual visitors to join the Trust or because such sites positively attract existing members of the Trust, perhaps on the grounds that they offer a particular 'bargain', or because price increases have occurred where members' visits have put pressure on sites. Little direct information to support these hypotheses can be obtained from the data base used in this study.

Analysis of the relationship between logged changes in real admission prices and logged changes in the ratio of paying visitors to members' visits shows that the relative growth of paying visits to members' visits over the two halves of the period studied was significantly correlated with changes in admission prices (Table 7.10). The price elasticity of this growth rate was -0.35 indicating that a 10% increase in real admission prices at a site will tend to bring a 3.5% decrease in the ratio of paying visits to members' visits.

The influence of location

The influences of site location on visitor trends over the decade can be seen most clearly in Tables 7.6 and 7.7 which analyse changes in the number of visits to DoE sites between the 1970-72 period and the 1978-79 period. For sites with high visitor numbers, and sites with high prices, urban locations were associated with very high increases in visitor numbers between these periods compared with the other categories of sites. However, there was a tendency for urban fringe sites to lose out relative to urban influenced and rural sites. This again demonstrates that the real increases in petrol price over the decade may have had short-term influences on recreation trip patterns, but the long-term influences may have been less straightforward and probably less important.

Table 7.9

Influences on the change in the number of visits by National Trust members between the 1970/75 period and the 1976/80 period

Conceptual Variables	Price	Locational Variables				Open Space Characteristics		Statistics	
Specific Measures / Equation Type	Adult Admission	Constant (Rural)	Urban	Urban Fringe <10 Miles	Urban Influence >10 <20 Miles	Gardens	Park	R^2	N Price
Percentage Change	0.89	169.6				−35.38	33.44	0.04	103
Absolute Change	21661**	2715	6566**			3448**	4262**	0.21	103
Log of Change	0.41*	3.54					0.10	0.04	103

Table 7.10

Influences on the change in the ratio of paying visits to members, visits between the 1970/75 period and the 1976/80 period

Conceptual Variables	Price		Locational Variables			Open Space Characteristics		Statistics	
Specific Measures / Equation Type	Adult Admission	Constant (Rural)	Urban	Urban Fringe <10 Miles	Urban Influence >10 <20 Miles	Gardens	Park	R^2	N Price
Percentage Change		0.05		−0.20*				0.05	74
Absolute Change	No significant equation							—	74
Log of Change	−0.35*	0.80			−0.10			0.06	74

The influence of property type

It is also clear from tables 7.6 and 7.7 that the only properties to be associated with a longer-term decline in visitor numbers were castles (and possibly priories). Tables 7.1 to 7.4 show that there were, however, substantial fluctuations in the number of visits to different types of property over shorter time periods. It has not been possible to identify factors influencing these shorter-term fluctuations.

The influence of parkland amenities

The sites in our data set which provide major parkland amenities are mainly National Trust sites. Consequently the poor performance of the longitudinal approach in estimating changes in the number of visitors to National Trust properties makes it difficult to come to conclusions about the longer-term influence of such amenities on visitor trends. The analysis indicated, however, that around 1970 sites with parks showed an above average growth in the number of visitors, but this trend was reversed in the period up to 1975. Thereafter, the regressions indicate that, as a group, sites with parkland amenities may have experienced visitor trends in line with National Trust sites as a whole.

Summary and conclusions

The longitudinal analysis of data for DoE sites suggested a range of price elasticities during the study period between -0.20 and -0.30. It appears that larger sites, at which prices were often increased most substantially, had rather higher elasticity values in 1978. However, there is no strong evidence that, over the 1970's as a whole, larger DoE sites became more price sensitive than sites with lower visitor numbers. The fact that these 'longer-term' elasticities appear rather lower than the year-on-year elasticities reported in Chapter 6, may indicate that the large scale price rises which were carried out every two or three years at DoE sites in the 1970's aroused relatively high short-term consumer resistance.

The longitudinal analysis of grouped data for National Trust sites did not provide such useful indicators of price elasticity as in the case of DoE sites. However, the influence of the growth in National Trust membership was highlighted by this analysis and there is an indication that price increases at individual sites can have a substantial effect on the proportion of visits to the site which come from members as opposed to paying visitors. This tendency is examined further in relation to specific sites in Chapter 8.

8 Time series analysis

Introduction

This chapter examines visitor trends over a number of years at a selection of DoE and National Trust sites. It addresses the questions:

(i) What are the price elasticites at individual sites?

(ii) Do elasticities differ between sites and, if so, is there any discernible pattern?

(iii) To what extent are admissions at individual sites influenced by other factors such as petrol prices, the state of the economy or the weather (and, at National Trust sites, by the growth of National Trust membership)?

Method of time series analysis

In order to estimate the elasticity of demand for visits to specific sites, changes in visitor numbers in individual months were regressed on changes in admission prices, controlling for changes in weather, travel costs, unemployment and inflation. Although the selection of sites for this analysis was partly dictated by data availability, as far as possible, sites were selected in order to reflect a range of recreational opportunities and locations as well as a range of admission price levels. Analysis was completed for twenty-two DoE sites using data collected for the period 1971-80 and for thirteen National Trust sites using data covering the period 1973-80. In order to take account of facilities which are closed to the public during the winter months, the analysis was confined to the period from April to September in each year. 'Dummy' variables were also incorporated to take account of the variable length of accounting periods and movable public holidays.

Price levels and changes

As was noted in Chapter 2, up until 1973, the admission charge at the majority of DoE sites was less than 10 pence (Table 8.1). Reviews of the level of charges which have taken place every 2 or 3 years have resulted in increases which, although modest in absolute terms, have often been substantial in percentage terms - averaging 28% in 1973; 103% in 1976; 41% in 1978; and 59% in 1980. In the intervening periods, inflation resulted in the gradual erosion of admission

Table 8.1

Cost of adult admission fee (pence) to Department of the Environment properties

Site	1970	1973	1976	1978	1980
Avebury	5	10	10	15	30
Lindisfarne	5	10	15	20	30
Orford	5	10	15	20	30
Whitby	5	10	15	20	30
Castle Acre	7.5	10	15	20	30
Fort	7.5	15	30	40	60
Framlingham	7.5	10	15	20	30
Goodrich	7.5	10	20	25	40
Housesteads	7.5	15	30	40	60
Kenilworth	7.5	15	25	30	40
Lullingstone	7.5	15	30	40	60
Richmond	7.5	10	15	20	30
Rievaulx	7.5	10	30	40	60
Scarborough	7.5	10	20	25	40
Walmer	7.5	10	30	40	60
Dover Castle	10	20	40	50	70
Stonehenge	10	20	40	40	40
Audley End	15	25	50	70	100
Carisbrooke	15	20	50	70	80
Fountains	15	20	40	50	70
Hampton Court	20	30	50	100	120
Osborne	20	25	50	70	100

Table 8.2

Real cost of admission to Department of the Environment properties (1970 prices) (figures rounded off)

Site	1970	1972	1973	1974	1975	1976	1977	1978	1979	1980
Avebury	5	4	8	8	6	5	4	6	5	8
Lindisfarne	5	4	8	7	6	7	6	8	7	8
Orford	5	4	8	7	6	7	6	8	7	8
Whitby	5	4	8	7	6	7	6	8	7	8
Castle Acre	8	7	8	7	6	7	6	8	7	8
Fort	8	7	12	10	9	14	12	15	14	17
Framlingham	8	7	8	7	6	7	6	8	7	8
Goodrich	8	7	8	7	6	10	8	9	9	11
Housesteads	8	7	12	10	9	14	12	15	14	17
Kenilworth	8	7	12	10	9	12	10	11	10	11
Lullingstone	8	7	12	10	9	14	12	15	14	17
Richmond	8	7	8	7	6	7	6	8	7	8
Rievaulx	8	7	8	7	6	14	12	15	14	17
Scarborough	8	7	8	7	6	10	8	9	9	11
Walmer	8	7	8	7	6	14	12	15	14	17
Dover Castle	10	9	16	14	11	19	16	19	17	20
Stonehenge	10	9	16	14	11	19	16	15	10	11
Audley End	15	13	20	17	14	24	20	26	24	28
Carisbrooke	15	13	16	14	11	24	20	26	24	23
Fountains	15	13	16	14	11	19	16	19	17	20
Hampton Court	20	17	24	21	17	24	20	38	34	34
Osborne	20	17	20	17	14	24	20	26	24	28

Table 8.3

Cost of adult admission fee (pence) to National Trust properties

Site	1970	1973	1974	1975	1976	1977	1978	1979	1980
Tatton Gardens	5	5	5	10	15	20	25	30	30
St. Michael's Mount	10	15	15	15	40	60	70	80	100
Shugborough	10	15	15	20	30	40	40	60	50
Tatton Hall	10	15	15	25	30	40	50	50	60
Chedworth	15	20	20	25	30	30	40	70	85
Packwood	20	30	30	40	50	50	60	70	85
Wallington	20	25	35	35	50	50	50	60	120
Hidcote	25	30	30	40	60	60	70	90	110
Knightshayes	25	30	30	60	70	80	80	100	130
Sheffield Park	25	25	30	40	70	70	70	80	100
Stourhead Gardens	25	30	40	40	60	60	60	60	80
Hardwick	30	30	50	50	80	90	100	100	120
Knole	30	35	40	40	70	70	80	100	120
Waddesdon	30	35	45	45	55	70	80	100	140

Table 8.4

Real cost of admission to National Trust properties (1970 prices)

Site	1970	1974	1975	1976	1977	1978	1979	1980
Tatton Gardens	5	3	6	7	8	9	9	8
St. Michael's Mount	10	10	9	19	24	26	27	28
Shugborough	10	10	11	14	16	15	21	14
Tatton Hall	10	10	14	14	16	19	17	17
Chedworth	15	14	14	14	12	15	24	24
Packwood	20	21	23	24	20	23	24	24
Wallington	20	24	20	24	20	19	21	34
Hidcote	25	21	23	29	24	26	31	31
Knightshayes	25	21	34	33	32	30	34	37
Sheffield Park	25	21	23	33	28	26	27	28
Stourhead Gardens	25	28	23	29	24	23	21	23
Hardwick	30	35	28	38	37	38	34	34
Knole	30	28	23	33	28	30	34	34
Waddesdon	30	31	26	26	28	30	34	39

Table 8.5

Cost of membership of National Trust

(a) Membership fee (Ordinary Adult — Pence)

	1973	1974	1975	1976	1977	1978	1979	1980
Money Cost	300	300	300	500	500	500	700	700
Real Cost (1970 prices)		207	170	238	203	188	239	197

(b) Admission Fee as a Percentage of Membership Fee (Selected Sites)

	1973	1974	1975	1976	1977	1978	1979	1980
Chedworth	6.7	6.7	8.3	6.0	6.0	8.0	10.0	12.1
Hidcote	10.0	10.0	13.3	12.0	12.0	14.0	12.8	15.7
Packwood	10.0	10.0	13.3	10.0	10.0	12.0	10.0	12.1
Shugborough	5.0	5.0	6.7	6.0	8.0	8.0	8.6	7.1
Tatton Hall	1.7	1.7	3.3	3.0	4.0	5.0	4.3	4.3
Tatton Gardens	5.0	5.0	8.3	6.0	8.0	10.0	7.1	8.6
Wallington	8.3	11.7	11.7	10.0	10.0	10.0	8.6	17.1

prices in real terms. Whilst in some instances these periodic increases did little more than restore real prices to their 1970 levels, in the case of some sites, such as Housesteads and Dover Castle, they resulted in a doubling of prices in real terms from 1971 to 1980 (Table 8.2).

Prices at National Trust sites have generally been maintained at a higher level than comparable DoE sites. Admission prices for individual properties have usually been reviewed annually by the regional administrators in the light of guidance and advice from the Trust's headquarters. Consequently, with few exceptions, there has been a more gradual increase in charges at individual sites and generally such increases have been kept in line with or slightly above the rate of inflation (Tables 8.3 and 8.4). Substantial increases in 1976, 1978, 1979 and 1980 have, however, resulted in admission charges for a few sites rising to as much as 70% above 1970 prices in real terms (Table 8.4). In a few cases, as at Chedworth Roman Villa and Wallington, these increases have occurred over a relatively short period of time. In many instances, admission charges have been set at levels which are likely to encourage visitors to become members of the Trust and thus gain 'free' access to all sites (Table 8.5).

Prices at Shugborough and Tatton Park, both of which are managed by County Councils, have been maintained at a lower level than comparable sites managed directly by the Trust itself, although price increases have been at similar rates.

The price-visitor relationship

In the first instance, the simple relationship between year-on-year changes in admision prices and changes in the number of paying visitors to each site was estimated - expressing change in both percentage and absolute terms (Tables 8.6 to 8.9). Subsequently, a range of other variables were included in the analysis. (Tables 8.10 to 8.17). For this time series analysis it was also possible to regress the actual number of visits against the admission price in each period (Tables 8.18 and 8.19).

DoE Sites

For thirteen of the twenty-two DoE sites studied, admission price was statistically significant and inversely correlated to variations in the number of visits in at least two of the estimating approaches used. For the other nine sites, admission price was either not strongly correlated with visitor numbers or the relationship was the reverse of that expected. These tended to be the cheaper sites. In the case of Housesteads and Lindisfarne, where price rises were significantly associated with increases in visitors, the influence of the strong promotion of these sites by the tourist authorities and their location in increasingly popular holiday areas may have largely explained the anomaly.

In the case of the thirteen sites with a significant price-visitor relationship, elasticity values were generally rather lower when estimated from the percentage change rather than the absolute change function (Table 8.21). For sites with a wide range of percentage price rises over the study period, the absolute change estimates of elasticity are more likely to be reliable. It should also be noted that the estimates included in the 'level' column in Table 8.21, derived from the analyses of the number of paying visits against the level of admission price in each month, are likely to be less reliable than the other

Table 8.6

Relationship between admission prices and number of paying visitors at National Trust sites

Site	Number of Observations	Percentage Change in Admission Price and Percentage Change in the Number of Paying Visitors				Change in Admission Price and Change in the Number of Paying Visitors			
		B Values	Significance * 95% **99%	R^2	Durbin Watson Statistic	**B Values**	Significance * 95% **99%	R^2	Durbin Watson Statistic
Tatton Gardens	40	**0.14**		0.24	2.0	**393.80**		0.12	1.9
St. Michael's Mount	40	**0.25**	**	0.26	1.9	**112.90**		0.06	0.8
Shugborough	40	**−0.30**	*	0.08	1.3	**−41.50**	**	0.18	1.7
Tatton Hall	40	**−0.05**		0.15	2.4	**−71.90**		0.11	2.5
Chedworth	34	**−0.17**		0.21	2.4	**−59.40**	*	0.17	2.5
Packwood	34	**−0.79**	*	0.42	2.0	**−10.00**		0.26	1.8
Wallington	40	**−0.14**		0.09	1.6	**−0.90**		0.07	1.3
Hidcote	34	**−0.85**	**	0.20	1.6	**−39.60**		0.04	1.8
Knightshayes	34	**−0.47**		0.09	1.4	—	—	—	—
Sheffield Park	40	**−0.51**	**	0.51	1.8	**−75.00**		0.19	1.7
Stourhead Gardens	40					**144.40**		0.13	1.7
Hardwick	34	**−0.09**		0.23	2.7	**−2.82**		0.22	2.8
Knole	37	**−0.13**		0.28	2.3	**−22.00**		0.19	2.3
Waddesdon	40	**−0.10**		0.24	2.4	**−11.80**		0.17	2.4

Table 8.7

Relationship between admission prices and number of paying visitors at DoE sites

		Percentage Change in Admission Price and Percentage Change in the Number of Paying Visitors				Change in Admission Price and Change in the Number of Paying Visitors			
Site	Number of Observations	**B Values**	Significance * 95% **99%	R^2	Durbin Watson Statistic	**B Values**	Significance * 95% **99%	R^2	Durbin Watson Statistic
Avebury	52	**-0.16**	*	0.12	1.33	**-64.5**	**	0.23	1.30
Lindisfarne	52	**0.80**	**	0.23	1.81	**-79.4**		0.19	1.35
Orford	52	**0.02**		0.07	2.25	**-12.9**	*	0.28	1.49
Whitby	52	**0.05**		0.06	1.73	**38.9**		0.23	1.31
Castle Acre	52	**0.37**		0.05	2.23	**4.4**		0.33	2.07
Fort	—	—	—	—	—	—	—	—	—
Framlingham	52	**0.14**		0.06	2.16	**32.4**		0.34	1.49
Goodrich	46	**-0.20**		0.16	2.13	**-20.8**		0.31	1.46
Housesteads	52	**0.11**		0.11	1.31	**-90.5**	**	0.28	1.35
Kenilworth	46	**-0.17**		0.07	2.35	**-104.4**	**	0.31	1.93
Lullingstone	50	**-0.13**	**	0.16	1.59	**-50.6**	**	0.51	1.42
Richmond	52	**-0.22**		0.10	1.60	**79.4**	*	0.24	1.46
Rievaulx	52	**-0.05**	*	0.15	2.12	**-27.4**	*	0.25	1.45
Scarborough	52	**-0.30**	**	0.24	1.78	**-211.7**	**	0.26	1.44
Walmer	52	**-0.07**	*	0.21	2.01	**-17.7**	*	0.27	1.39
Dover Castle	52	**-0.10**		0.11	2.04	**-157.9**	**	0.24	1.45
Stonehenge	52	**0.03**		0.02	1.61	**-4.7**		0.15	1.33
Audley End	52	**0.03**		0.11	2.02	**-30.6**	**	0.59	1.53
Carisbrooke	52	**-0.33**	*	0.09	2.29	**-113.9**	**	0.29	1.58
Fountains	52	**-0.13**		0.05	1.43	**-43.0**		0.17	1.56
Hampton Court	46	**-0.14**		0.05	2.76	**-161.6**	**	0.21	1.95
Osborne	50	**-0.60**	**	0.34	1.97	**60.1**	*	0.21	1.63

Table 8.8

Relationship between real admission prices and number of paying visitors at National Trust sites

		Percentage Change in Real Admission Price and Percentage Change in the Number of Paying Visitors				Change in Real Admission Price and Change in the Number of Paying Visitors			
Site	Number of Observations	**B Values**	Significance * 95% **99%	R^2	Durbin Watson Statistic	**B Values**	Significance * 95% **99%	R^2	Durbin Watson Statistic
Tatton Gardens	40	**0.25**		0.24	2.0	**480.4**		0.11	1.8
St. Michael's Mount	40	**0.29**		0.28	2.0	**552.1**	**	0.28	1.2
Shugborough	40	**−0.38**		0.10	1.3	**−97.3**	**	0.14	1.3
Tatton Hall	40	**−0.01**		0.15	2.4	**−150.9**		0.11	2.5
Chedworth	34	**−0.19**		0.22	2.5	**−170.1**	*	0.16	2.4
Packwood	34	**−0.97**	*	0.42	2.0	**−80.0**		0.33	1.9
Wallington	40	**−0.17**		0.09	1.6	**−17.0**		0.09	1.4
Hidcote	34	**−1.03**	**	0.22	1.6	**−181.0**		0.09	1.9
Knightshayes	34	**−0.65**		0.03	1.5	**−69.8**		0.07	1.7
Sheffield Park	40	**−0.53**	*	0.49	1.7	**−220.1**	*	0.22	1.8
Stourhead Gardens	40	**0.21**		0.26	1.9	**186.1**		0.08	1.7
Hardwick	34	**−0.06**		0.23	2.7	**−3.8**		0.22	2.8
Knole	37	**−0.10**		0.28	2.3	**−27.7**	*	0.18	2.3
Waddesdon	40	**−0.09**		0.24	2.4	**−13.7**		0.17	2.4

Table 8.9

Relationship between real admission prices and number of paying visitors at DoE sites

Site	Number of Observations	Percentage Change in Real Admission Price and Percentage Change in the Number of Paying Visitors				Change in Real Admission Price and Change in the Number of Paying Visitors			
		B Values	Significance * 95% **99%	R^2	Durbin Watson Statistic	B Values	Significance * 95% **99%	R^2	Durbin Watson Statistic
Avebury	52	-0.15	*	0.10	1.30	-97.80		0.07	1.31
Lindisfarne	52	0.89	**	0.25	1.87	-562.76	**	0.13	1.59
Orford	52	0.02		0.07	2.25	3.00		0.05	1.97
Whitby	52	0.06		0.07	1.74	26.20		0.02	0.02
Castle Acre	52	0.48		0.06	1.53	152.50		0.04	2.13
Fort	52	—	—	—	—	—	—	—	—
Framlingham	52	0.13		0.06	2.14	-41.10		0.08	1.84
Goodrich	46	-0.23	**	0.17	2.14	-184.20	**	0.10	2.01
Housesteads	52	0.16	*	0.13	1.36	118.10		0.05	1.36
Kenilworth	46	-0.20		0.08	2.35	213.50		0.04	2.53
Lullingstone	50	-0.14	*	0.15	1.56	-72.70	**	0.16	1.41
Richmond	52	-0.26	*	0.11	1.60	-139.40		0.03	1.54
Rievaulx	52	-0.16		0.15	2.11	-63.80		0.08	1.80
Scarborough	52	-0.30	**	0.21	1.71	-586.20	**	0.27	1.40
Walmer	52	-0.09	**	0.21	2.02	-50.10	**	0.18	1.72
Dover Castle	52	-0.10		0.11	1.43	-223.10	*	0.11	1.95
Stonehenge	52	0.05		0.02	1.62	200.80		0.01	1.54
Audley End	52	0.06		0.12	2.00	21.20		0.12	1.94
Carisbrooke	52	-0.36	*	0.08	2.29	-473.70	**	0.25	2.56
Fountains	52	-0.14		0.04	1.43	-225.50		0.04	1.65
Hampton Court	46	-0.14		0.05	2.75	-360.00		0.04	2.86
Osborne	50	-0.64	**	0.33	1.97	-699.10	**	0.29	2.36

estimates, because of the absence of monthly dummy variables.

From Table 8.21 it can be seen that elasticity values for DoE sites vary considerably. Taking only estimates from the absolute change and percentage change functions, low values appear to have characterized Walmer Castle (-0.07 to -0.18) Lullingstone Roman Villa (-0.13 to -0.21), and Avebury (-0.15 to -0.20). Medium elasticity values were found at Dover Castle (-0.20 to -0.30), Goodrich Castle (-0.23 to -0.32) and Scarborough Castle (-0.30 to -0.36). Finally, relatively high elasticity values were found at Carisbrooke Castle (-0.36 to -0.63) and Osborne House (-0.55 to -0.64). These elasticity values seem in general to be lower than at comparable National Trust sites; this is almost certainly attributable to the fact that admission prices at DoE sites were maintained at a relatively low level throughout this period.

National Trust sites

All except three of the National Trust sites included in this analysis showed the expected negative relationship between changes in the number of visitors and changes in admission prices (Table 8.6). The summary table for these simple price-visitor regressions (Table 8.21) shows that in the majority of cases, the relationship was weak; and only in six cases (a lower proportion than for DoE sites) was price statistically significant in more than one of the estimating approaches adopted. In these cases, the elasticity values estimated ranged from quite low values at Chedworth Roman Villa (between -0.36 and -0.49), Shugborough (between -0.30 and -0.59), and Waddesdon Manor (-0.21 to -0.59), through medium values at Sheffield Park (-0.51 to -0.91) and up to high values at Packwood House (-0.79 to -1.00) and Hidcote Manor Garden (-0.85 to -1.03).

The higher end of the range of elasticity values for Chedworth, Shugborough, Waddesdon and Sheffield Park was derived from the regressions of absolute levels of visits against admission prices. These regressions, without the monthly 'dummy' variables, whose effects are reported in the next section, must be regarded as less reliable than the other equations in Table 8.6, so that for these four sites, the figures at the lower end of the range must be regarded as more reliable estimates of the price elasticity value.

The other nine National Trust sites did not, however, demonstrate significant correlations between changes in admission prices and changes in the number of visitors. Indeed, price rises appeared to be associated with increases in visitor numbers at Stourhead, Tatton Park and St. Michael's Mount. In the case of St. Michael's Mount this probably reflects the improvements to facilities and the promotion of the site which have been associated with the development of the Country Park.

The influence of other variables on the price-visitor relationship

Tables 8.10 to 8.19 show the results of extending the analysis to include other variables such as car running costs, unemployment, average earnings and monthly 'dummies' acting as proxies for holiday periods and seasonal supply factors (such as 'blossom time', or major events held annually in specific months). The regressions in Tables 8.18 and 8.19 relate the actual number of visitors in each month to the real admission price, economic indices, weather variables and monthly 'dummy' variables. They, therefore, show up the monthly

Table 8.10

Relationship between % change in admission prices and % change in number of paying visitors at National Trust sites

Conceptual Variables	Price	Weather Indices		Economic Indices				Statistics		
Specific Measures / Site	Adult Admission Price	Sunshine Level	Rain Days	Car Running Cost	Average Earnings (Regional)	Unem-ployment (Regional)	Time Trend	R^2	N	Durbin Watson
Tatton Gardens		0.62		−0.67				0.29	40	2.00
St. Michael's Mount	0.18*		−0.13**	−0.37**			−0.22*	0.47	40	2.50
Shugborough	−0.37**		−0.07*	−0.46**		0.29**		0.35	40	1.78
Tatton Hall					−0.77			0.16	40	2.26
Chedworth		−0.25	−0.06*			0.19*		0.35	34	2.29
Packwood	−1.05*					0.21	0.50**	0.51	34	2.36
Wallington			0.07	−0.40**				0.22	40	2.01
Hidcote	−0.96**			0.42				0.25	34	1.71
Knightshayes		1.33		−1.90				0.23	34	1.81
Sheffield Park	−0.61**		−0.08*					0.55	40	2.09
Stourhead Gardens					3.49**		1.10**	0.40	40	2.15
Hardwick	−0.26	−0.56**	−0.05*					0.39	34	2.50
Knole	−0.21			−0.37*				0.33	37	2.45
Waddesdon							0.13	0.26	40	2.75

Table 8.11

Relationship between change in admission prices and change in number of paying visitors at National Trust sites

Conceptual Variables	Price	Weather Indices		Economic Indices				Statistics		
Specific Measures / Site	Adult Admission Price	Sunshine Level	Rain Days	Car Running Cost	Average Earnings (Regional)	Unemployment (Regional)	Time Trend	R^2	N	Durbin Watson
Tatton Gardens	464.5	72.9*						0.19	40	2.16
St. Michael's Mount	94.5		-288.2**	-37.9**				0.46	40	1.53
Shugborough	-44.3**		-42.5**	-5.5*				0.33	40	1.52
Tatton Hall						-480.3		0.12	40	2.51
Chedworth	-60.5*		-98.3**					0.29	34	2.32
Packwood	-32.6*		-15.2				12.44**	0.49	34	2.36
Wallington	-14.4**		22.7*	-4.2**	82.2**		5.60	0.35	40	1.79
Hidcote	-59.7			14.6*		-413.7		0.15	34	2.06
Knightshayes	-63.2**		-75.8**		53.5			0.31	34	1.85
Sheffield Park	-140.1**		-155.8**		111.0		38.10*	0.39	40	2.43
Stourhead Gardens			-252.8**		371.3**	-967.4		0.32	40	2.12
Hardwick		-1.7				13.2		0.26	34	2.71
Knole			-64.3	-13.0*				0.28	37	2.64
Waddesdon										

Table 8.12

Relationship between % change in real admission prices and % change in number of paying visitors at National Trust sites

Conceptual Variables	Price	Weather Indices		Economic Indices				Statistics		
Specific Measures / Site	Adult Admission Price	Sunshine Level	Rain Days	Average Earnings (Regional)	Unem-ployment (Regional)	Car Running Cost	Time Trend	R^2	N	Durbin Watson
Tatton Gardens		0.42						0.26	40	1.96
St. Michael's Mount	0.23**		−0.14**	−0.87		−0.28	−0.26*	0.50	40	2.51
Shugborough	−0.43**		−0.07*		0.20**	−0.70**		0.38	40	1.80
Tatton Hall				−0.74				0.17	40	2.24
Chedworth			−0.05		−0.16			0.31	34	2.29
Packwood	−0.93**					−0.22	0.45**	0.52	34	2.50
Wallington	−0.28*		0.07	1.16*		−0.52**	0.42**	0.23	40	2.05
Hidcote	−1.02**					0.34		0.24	34	1.72
Knightshayes		1.23*				−2.41**		0.20	34	1.82
Sheffield Park	−0.69**		−0.08*			−0.29		0.54	40	2.05
Stourhead Gardens		0.64		3.11*			1.14**	0.43	40	2.10
Hardwick	−0.30	−0.59**	−0.05*					0.40	34	2.52
Knole	−0.26		−0.04			−0.55*		0.35	37	2.43
Waddesdon							0.13	0.26	40	2.75

Table 8.13

Relationship between change in real admission prices and change in number of paying visitors at National Trust sites

Conceptual Variables	Price	Weather Indices		Economic Indices				Statistics		
Specific Measures / Site	Adult Admission Price	Sunshine Level	Rain Days	Average Earnings (Regional)	Unem-ployment (Regional)	Car Running Cost	Time Trend	R^2	N	Durbin Watson
Tatton Gardens		-94.9**				-127.8		0.22	40	2.34
St. Michael's Mount	584.3**	35.2	-209.7**	-250.8**				0.55	40	1.72
Shugborough	-121.8**		-41.1**			-25.6**		0.37	40	1.59
Tatton Hall					-480.3			0.12	40	2.63
Chedworth	-167.7*		-95.8**		-0.16			0.28	34	2.29
Packwood	-80.3**		-18.2*			-10.4**	11.0**	0.55	34	2.50
Wallington	-40.0**		23.7*	64.4**		-14.3**		0.41	40	1.89
Hidcote	-181.0							0.09	34	2.07
Knightshayes			-84.3**		-220.3	-34.5**		0.26	34	1.87
Sheffield Park	-237.6**		-153.5**			-28.4	33.8*	0.37	40	2.37
Stourhead Gardens			-252.8**	371.3**	-957.4			0.27	40	2.13
Hardwick		-11.4						0.28	34	2.69
Knole			-57.2			-46.2**		0.30	37	2.73
Waddesdon			-50.3					0.19	40	2.70

Table 8.14

Relationship between % change in number of paying visitors and % change in admission prices at DoE sites

Conceptual Variables	Price	Weather Indices		Economic Indices			Statistics		
Specific Measures / Site	Adult Admission Price	Sunshine Level	Rain Days	Petrol Costs	Average Earnings (Regional)	Unemployment (Regional)	R^2	N	Durbin Watson
Avebury	−0.17**			−0.39**	−0.03		0.25	52	1.6
Lindisfarne	0.57**					−1.05**	0.32	52	2.2
Orford						−0.05	0.08	52	2.4
Whitby		0.26**		−0.29**			0.21	52	2.2
Castle Acre			−0.14				0.05	52	2.5
Framlingham		−0.16					0.07	52	2.2
Goodrich	−0.23**		−0.05**				0.25	46	2.4
Housesteads				−0.28**		−0.50**	0.33	52	1.9
Kenilworth		0.64**			−4.30**	0.53**	0.32	46	2.5
Lullingstone	−0.16**			−0.14			0.18	52	1.7
Richmond				−0.35**			0.16	52	2.0
Rievaulx			−0.07**		−0.6*		0.24	52	2.2
Scarborough	−0.25**					−0.19	0.28	52	2.0
Walmer	−0.09**	−0.19	−0.06*	0.30**			0.33	52	1.8
Dover Castle	−0.09				−0.70*		0.18	52	2.2
Stonehenge				−0.35**	−0.68		0.24	52	2.1
Audley End			−0.06*	−0.24*			0.20	52	2.4
Carisbrooke	−0.33						0.08	52	2.2
Fountains		0.57**				−0.36**	0.25	52	1.7
Hampton Court	−0.09	−0.30*					0.10	46	3.1
Osborne	−0.54**		0.07*				0.38	50	2.0

Table 8.15

Relationship between % change in number of paying visitors and % change in real admission prices at DoE sites

Conceptual Variables	Price	Weather Indices		Economic Indices				Statistics		
Specific Measures / Site	Adult Admission Price	Sunshine Level	Rain Days	Petrol Costs	Average Earnings (Regional)	Unem-ployment (Regional)	Car Running Costs	R^2	N	Durbin Watson
Avebury	−0.19**				−0.37		−0.58**	0.26	52	1.7
Lindisfarne	0.61**					−0.95**		0.32	52	2.2
Orford						−0.06		0.08	52	2.4
Whitby		0.24**			−0.74*			0.20	52	2.2
Castle Acre	−0.47							0.06	52	2.5
Fort		0.23**					−0.68**	0.24	52	2.1
Framlingham		−0.16	−0.08					0.07	52	2.1
Goodrich	−0.35**		−0.06**				−0.40*	0.32	46	2.5
Housesteads		0.13				−0.54**	−0.47**	0.35	52	1.9
Kenilworth		0.52**				0.25**		0.32	46	2.4
Lullingstone	−0.18**						−0.27	0.19	52	1.8
Richmond	−0.3*		−0.05		1.11*	−0.26**	−0.03	0.17	52	1.9
Rievaulx			−0.07**		−0.60*			0.24	52	2.2
Scarborough	−0.25**	0.15				−0.23*		0.26	52	1.9
Walmer	−0.10**	−0.18	−0.05**				0.37**	0.26	52	1.8
Dover Castle	−0.10				−0.75**			0.18	52	2.2
Stonehenge					−0.76*		−0.56**	0.27	52	2.1
Audley End			−0.07*			−0.08	−0.33*	0.22	52	2.4
Carisbrooke	−0.37*							0.10	52	2.2
Fountains		0.57**				−0.36**		0.25	52	1.7
Hampton Court	−0.22*	−0.19					−0.52	0.16	46	3.1
Osborne	−0.57**		0.06					0.37	50	2.0

Table 8.16

Relationship between change in number of visits and change in admission prices at DoE sites

Conceptual Variables	Price	Weather Indices		Economic Indices			Statistics		
Specific Measures / Site	Adult Admission Price	Sunshine Level	Rain Days	Petrol Costs	Average Earnings (Regional)	Unem-ployment (Regional)	R^2	N	Durbin Watson
Avebury					-68.5**	170.7	0.21	52	1.6
Lindisfarne	127.9		82.7*			-1049.8**	0.28	52	1.9
Orford				2.1			0.11	52	2.2
Whitby		9.8				-522.9**	0.17	52	1.5
Castle Acre		-11.7	-74.8**				0.12	52	2.3
Fort		11.0		-14.0**			0.11	52	1.3
Framlingham		-15.9**	-52.1**	9.9**	-54.2*		0.28	52	2.1
Goodrich	-54.1**		-47.1**				0.26	46	2.1
Housesteads	92.9**				-223.1**	-295.8	0.39	52	1.6
Kenilworth	-130.1*	-164.5*	-177.1				0.26	46	2.4
Lullingstone	-27.7*						0.14	52	1.5
Richmond	-97.4				89.6*		0.10	52	1.7
Rievaulx			-67.5**		-74.8**		0.25	52	1.9
Scarborough	-180.3**	14.1*				-535.4**	0.43	52	1.9
Walmer	-30.9**			7.0**			0.32	52	1.5
Dover Castle	-147.6**		78.1				0.17	52	2.1
Stonehenge				-96.0**			0.16	52	2.0
Audley End			-52.1		-93.9**		0.28	52	2.5
Carisbrooke	-220.7**		81.7				0.26	52	2.5
Fountains		62.0**				-1905.8**	0.20	52	1.9
Hampton Court			693.8**				0.11	46	3.2
Osborne	-225.4**	-115.1**					0.45	50	2.6

Table 8.17

Relationship between change in number of visits and change in real admission prices at DoE sites

Conceptual Variables	Price	Weather Indices			Economic Indices			Statistics		
Specific Measures / Site	Adult Admission Price	Sunshine Level	Rain Days	Petrol Costs	Average Earnings (Regional)	Unem-ployment (Regional)	Car Running Costs	R^2	N	Durbin Watson
Avebury	-103.4				-31.6		-22.3**	0.25	52	1.7
Lindisfarne	373.5*		76.0*			-831.4**		0.31	52	2.0
Orford			-15.6					0.08	52	2.1
Whitby	-218.1*	16.6**				-608.1**	-47.0**	0.30	52	1.7
Castle Acre		-11.7	-74.8**					0.12	52	2.3
Fort		12.8					-64.0**	0.19	52	1.6
Framlingham		-16.7**	-55.6**				19.2*	0.23	52	2.1
Goodrich	-182.9**	47.6**					-13.0	0.33	46	2.4
Housesteads	179.7**		-43.0		-204.8**		-13.0	0.35	52	1.6
Kenilworth	-435.7**	50.5**	-118.9				-60.4	0.29	46	2.4
Lullingstone	-98.6**						-13.2*	0.20	50	1.7
Richmond							34.4**	0.13	52	1.7
Rievaulx			-67.5**		-74.8**			0.25	52	1.9
Scarborough	-372.9**	14.8*				-637.4**		0.47	52	1.8
Walmer	-59.8**						15.8**	0.30	52	1.9
Dover Castle	-219.3*					-942.7*	-52.5	0.16	52	2.1
Stonehenge					-347.2		-343.8**	0.27	52	2.1
Audley End			-52.1		-93.9**			0.28	52	2.5
Carisbrooke	-480.2**				-83.3			0.27	52	2.6
Fountains		62.0*				-1905.8**		0.20	52	1.9
Hampton Court	-642.8*		576.7*				-334.2*	0.19	46	3.3
Osborne	-844.9**	-78.6**					-166.6**	0.50	50	2.7

Table 8.18

Relationship between real admission prices and number of paying visitors at National Trust sites

Conceptual Variables	Price	Weather Indices		Economic Indices					Monthly Variation in Visitor Levels					Statistics		
Specific Measures / Sites	Adult Admission Price	Sunshine Level	Rain Days	Petrol Costs	Retail Price Index	Average Earnings (Regional)	Unemployment (Regional)	Time Trend	May	June	July	Aug.	Sept.	R^2	N	Durbin Watson
Tatton Gardens										11188.3 **	9433.2 **	5078.8 **	5269.3	0.51	40	2.61
St. Michael's Mount	661.7 **		−275.6 **			−67.6				9411.5 **	19766.1 **	28432.7 **	11819.0 **	0.92	40	1.49
Shugborough	−85.1 **		55.3 **	−6.5 **			149.4 *			−2013.2 **	−1092.6 **	2134.0 **	−2240.7 **	0.90	40	1.91
Tatton Hall	−252.4										3348.8 **	8564.9 **		0.51	40	2.61
Chedworth	−248.3 **		−50.8							4511.0 **	7302.2 **	1972.1 **	2586.2 **	0.85	34	2.37
Packwood	−55.5		−13.5						−454.8 **	349.8 **	821.0 **			0.69	34	2.11
Wallington				−3.6		9.4			−2904.8		1329.9			0.89	40	2.25
Hidcote				6.7 *						4605.6 **	6524.3 **		2213.4 **	0.76	34	1.72
Knightshayes	−390.9 **		−31.8			63.6 **	−526.6 **						−854.3 **	0.72	34	2.34
Sheffield Park	−311.1 *		−217.1 **				−736.0			6692.0 **		−2605.2 **		0.83	40	1.91
Stourhead Gardens	342.4 *		−287.3 **	26.0 **			1344.3 **			8411.9 **	2074.7	−10752 **		0.81	40	1.77
Hardwick	−37.9	−11.8	−47.2 *							1410.1 *	550.3 **	2421.1 **	1347 *	0.70	34	2.81
Knole	−113.1 *			−20.5 **				72.6 **		2889.5 **	5023.1 **	4818.4 **	3007.6 **	0.84	37	2.24
Waddesdon			−106.3 *			−35.9 **			−5242.3 **	1193.9 *	2462.0 **			0.82	40	2.75

Table 8.19

Relationship between admission prices and number of paying visitors at National Trust sites

Conceptual Variables	Price	Weather Indices		Economic Indices					Monthly Variation in Visitor Levels					Statistics		
Specific Measures / Sites	Adult Admission Price	Sunshine Level	Rain Days	Petrol Costs	Retail Price Index	Average Earnings (Regional)	Unemployment (Regional)	Time Trend	May	June	July	Aug.	Sept.	R^2	N	Durbin Watson
Tatton Gardens										11188.3 **	9433.2 **	5078.8 **	5269.3	0.51	40	2.60
St. Michael's Mount	304.6 **		-294.3 *			-296.5 **	528.7			9335.8 **	19223.2 **	27618.3 **	11092.8 **	0.93	40	1.45
Shugborough	-24.1 **		-52.1 **	-4.5 **			143.7			-1992.0 **	-1072.1 **	2154.3 **	-2209.5 **	0.89	40	1.89
Tatton Hall				8.9			-668.5 *			4448.3 **	7067.3 **	9569.2 **	3624.4 *	0.69	40	2.87
Chedworth	-49.9 **		-50.4							4649.1 **	7507.6 **	2105.8 **	2840.7 **	0.85	34	2.43
Packwood								-3.34	-512.8 **	372.3 **	871.7 **			0.67	34	2.14
Wallington				-1.0					-2879.7 **		1312.8 **			0.89	40	2.23
Hidcote	-130.5 **			19.6 **				72.9 *		4677.0 **	6443.0 *		2074.4 **	0.71	34	1.72
Knightshayes	-146.3 **		-37.7		24.0	141.1 *	-504.5 **						-688.2 *	0.71	34	2.57
Sheffield Park	-69.6		-175.1 **	17.1 *			-1165.8 *			6540.6 **		-2241.2 *		0.83	40	2.10
Stourhead Gardens			-267.1 **				-724.9 *			9099.4 **	2608.6	-11212.0 **		0.81	40	1.88
Hardwick		-7.9	-56.8							1372.0 **	1723.0 **	2446.1 **	1287.4 **	0.77	34	2.80
Knole	-49.2 *		-30.6	-25.9 **	46.4 **					2587.9 **	4764.2 **	4851.4 **	2882.1 **	0.85	34	2.26
Waddesdon			-110.7 **		-14.0 **				-5341.8 **	1123.4 *	2445.0 **			0.82	40	2.73

variations in admissions in a way which the analyses of percentage change and absolute change cannot, since these latter approaches always compare variables in the same month but one year apart.

Two interesting results emerge from these regressions. Firstly, at almost all National Trust and DoE sites at least one (and usually several) of the monthly 'dummies' was highly significant. In most cases this reflected a high seasonality in paying admissions. Secondly, the significant months differed considerably from site to site, although August was the most common. This indicates that demand peaks were not simply due to the good weather associated with summer months and that, even if price elasticities in general were high, there might be room for substantial price differention between peak and other summer months. It does not, of course, provide evidence on whether or not price elasticity is actually higher or lower in the peak months, which is an important issue in deciding whether price differentiation should involve offering off-peak concessions or imposing a premium at peak periods. This issue is discussed further in Chapter 10.

When account was taken of other variables, the significance of changes in admission prices at National Trust sites was generally enhanced for those sites which showed a significant relationship in the simple regression analysis. Elasticity values derived from these analyses were generally very similar to those estimated by the simpler equations. However, the values estimated from changes in the number of visits with changes in real admission prices at Sheffield Park (-0.61 to -0.70) and Shugborough (-0.35 to -0.45) were slightly higher when account was taken of changes in travel costs and weather (Tables 8.10 to 8.13). In addition, change in real admission prices appeared as a significant influence on changes in the number of paying visitors at Wallington, with an elasticity value of around -0.30, and just short of significant at Knole and Hardwick Hall, with values ranging from -0.21 to -0.30 (Tables 8.10 and 8.12).

When other variables were included in the analysis of changes in the number of visitors at DoE sites, the significance of admission price changes generally increased slightly (Tables 8.14 to 8.17). Elasticity values were broadly similar to those derived from the simpler equations, although slightly lower in the case of Scarborough Castle (-0.25) and Walmer Castle (-0.10), and slightly higher in the case of Avebury (-0.20), Lullingstone Roman Villa (-0.18) and Osborne House (-0.70). Changes in real prices also now appeared as a significant influence on changes in visits to Hampton Court (-0.20 to -0.30), Kenilworth Castle (-0.50), and Richmond Castle (-0.30).

The influence of other variables on the number of visits

The most significant influences on changes in the number of visits to National Trust sites appeared to be changes in the weather and the running costs of private cars. Thus, not suprisingly, sites with extensive gardens or parklands showed a significant tendency for the number of visits to drop with an increase in the number of rain days and to rise with an increase in the amount of sunshine. Several of the more remote sites, such as Wallington and St. Michael's Mount, have also shown a significant tendency for the number of visits to drop as petrol prices and the running costs of private cars have risen (Tables 8.12 and 8.13).

Changes in the number of visitors to several DoE sites were also significantly related to changes in a range of economic indicators. Again the most significant of these, particularly for the more remote rural sites and several of those in holiday areas, was the change in the running costs of private cars. Thus, increases in the price of petrol or car running costs showed a significant correlation with decreases in the number of paying visitors to such sites as Audley End, Avebury, Goodrich Castle, Housesteads, Richmond Castle, Stonehenge and Whitby Abbey (Tables 8.14 and 8.17). In addition, the number of paying admissions to some sites, particularly Housesteads and Fountains Abbey, in the north of England, have tended to decline as regional unemployment levels have risen.

As in the case of National Trust sites, variations in the weather between years also appear to have had a significant influence on changes in the number of visitors to DoE properties. Generally, increases in the amount of sunshine tended to be correlated with increases in the number of visitors and increases in the incidence of rain days with decreases. On the other hand, visits to Hampton Court and some other sites in holiday areas, such as Osborne House and Carisbrooke Castle, showed a tendency to rise with increases in the number of rain days and to fall off with increases in the amount of sunshine.

Visits by National Trust members

Despite the tendency for the number of paying visitors to National Trust sites to decline with increases in admission charges, the total numbers of visitors to individual sites have generally not fallen to the same extent. The balance has generally been made up by a steady growth in the number of visits made by National Trust members.

As was noted above, in several instances admission charges to the more popular National Trust sites have been set at levels which are likely to encourage visitors to become members of the Trust (Table 8.5). Thus, we would expect the proportion of visits made by members to increase as admission prices increase relative to the membership fee. Generally speaking this does in fact appear to have occurred, and all except four of the sites examined showed a significant positive correlation between the ratio of admission prices to membership fee and the ratio of members' visits to paying visitors (Table 8.20(a)). This statistical relationship is, however, largely attributable to the strong time trend in the data - reflecting, amongst other things, the strong growth in the number of National Trust members, especially towards the end of the period studied. When account is taken of this trend, the ratio of admission prices to membership fee appears to have had a significant positive influence on the ratio of members' visits to paying visits in only three cases, although it was almost significant in two other cases. (Table 8.20(b)). Not surprisingly, these tended to be those sites, such as Waddesdon and Wallington, which had the highest entrance charges and where real prices increased substantially towards the end of this period. It would appear therefore, that increases in admission charges at these sites may have encouraged potential paying visitors to opt for membership of the Trust.

Table 8.20

Relationship between ratio of National Trust members' visits to paying visits and ratio of entrance fee to membership fee

(a) Simple bi-variate

Site	R Squared	B Values	N	Durbin Watson
Chedworth	0.66	3.49**	34	1.00
Hardwick	0.02	1.32	33	0.70
Hidcote	0.32	13.79**	34	1.10
Knightshayes	0.03	−4.80	34	1.20
Knole	0.64	13.28**	37	1.10
Packwood	0.05	−3.4	34	0.70
St. Michael's Mount	0.43	2.48**	40	0.90
Sheffield Park	0.16	6.17*	40	0.80
Shugborough	0.32	12.48**	40	0.30
Stourhead Gardens	0.17	−6.46**	40	1.40
Tatton Gardens	0.35	3.99**	37	1.00
Tatton Hall	0.29	3.27**	37	0.90
Waddesdon	0.43	3.86**	40	0.53
Wallington	0.16	4.89	40	1.00

(b) Incorporating Time Trend

Site	R Squared	B Values		N	Durbin Watson
Chedworth	0.79	TIME CM	0.24** 1.80**	34	1.7
Hardwick	0.68	TIME CM	0.68** 1.59	33	2.2
Hidcote	0.49	TIME CM	0.79** 5.89	34	1.6
Knightshayes	0.03	CM	−4.80	34	1.2
Knole	0.84	TIME	0.77**	37	1.7
Packwood	0.56	TIME CM	0.71** −1.23	34	1.6
St. Michael's Mount	0.52	TIME	0.41**	40	1.0
Sheffield Park	0.61	TIME	0.71**	40	1.2
Shugborough	0.84	TIME CM	1.15** −5.55*	40	1.2
Stourhead Gardens	0.28	TIME	0.47*	40	1.6
Tatton Gardens	0.66	TIME	0.24**	37	1.6
Tatton Hall	0.75	TIME	0.31**	37	2.4
Waddesdon	0.86	TIME CM	0.46** 1.43**	40	1.6
Wallington	0.61	TIME CM	0.88** 1.26*	40	2.3

Table 8.21

Estimates of price elasticity of demand for visits to sites derived from simple regressions

(a) National Trust Sites

Sites	**Money Prices**			**Real Prices**		
	Level	Absolute Change	% Change	Level	Absolute Change	% Change
Chedworth	—	-0.36	—	-0.49	-0.36	—
Hardwick	—	-0.06	—	—	—	—
Hidcote	—	—	-0.85	—	—	-1.03
Knightshayes	-0.88	—	—	—	—	—
Knole	—	—	—	—	-0.12	—
Packwood	—	—	-0.79	—	-1.00	-0.97
St. Michael's Mount	—	—	—	—	—	—
Sheffield Park	—	—	-0.51	-0.91	-0.51	-0.53
Shugborough	-0.37	-0.45	-0.30	-0.59	-0.41	—
Stourhead Gardens	—	—	—	—	—	—
Tatton Gardens	—	—	—	—	—	—
Tatton Hall	—	—	—	—	—	—
Waddesdon	-0.21	—	—	-0.59	—	—
Wallington	—	—	—	—	—	—

(b) D.O.E. Sites

Sites	**Money Prices**			**Real Prices**		
	Level	Absolute Change	% Change	Level	Absolute Change	% Change
Audley End	-0.16	—	—	-0.29	—	—
Avebury	-0.21	-0.20	-0.16	-0.36	—	-0.15
Carisbrook	-0.04	-0.63	-0.33	-0.66	-0.55	-0.36
Castle Acre	—	—	—	-0.14	—	—
Chesters Roman Fort	—	—	—	-0.18	—	—
Dover Castle	-0.33	-0.30	—	-0.64	-0.20	—
Fountains	—	—	—	—	—	—
Framlingham	—	—	—	-0.07	—	—
Goodrich	—	—	—	-0.31	-0.32	-0.23
Hampton Court	-0.17	—	—	—	—	—
Housesteads	-0.27	—	—	-0.47	0.16	—
Kenilworth	-0.31	—	—	-0.65	—	—
Lindisfarne	—	—	—	—	—	—
Lullingstone	-0.36	-0.19	-0.13	-0.77	-0.21	-0.14
Orford	-0.04	—	—	-0.10	—	—
Osborne	—	-0.55	-0.60	—	-0.62	-0.64
Richmond	-0.16	—	—	-0.30	—	-0.26
Rievaulx	-0.08	—	-0.05	—	—	—
Scarborough	-0.30	-0.35	-0.30	-0.08	-0.36	-0.30
Stonehenge	—	—	—	—	—	—
Walmer	-0.15	-0.12	-0.07	-0.28	-0.18	-0.09
Whitby	—	—	—	—	—	—

Summary and conclusions

Where the regressions with a wider range of independent variables gave significant price elasticities for sites, these are generally to be preferred to the results of the simpler bi-variate analyses. In Table 8.22 we summarise the preferred estimates of price elasticity for each of the National Trust and DoE sites for which admission prices appeared as statistically significant in at least two of the percentage change and/or absolute change regressions. For both National Trust and DoE sites, a wide range of elasticities was found. DoE sites do seem, however, to have had lower elasticities than National Trust sites during this period. This is in line with the results of the very different statistical approaches discussed in Chapters 6 and 7. For sites which have in recent years sharply increased their admission prices in real terms or greatly extended their visitor attractions or promotions, these elasticity values may be only of historical interest. However, for many sites they should indicate approximately their remaining potential for increasing revenue by raising admission prices.

There is no clear pattern evident in the list of National Trust or DoE sites for which admission prices do not appear to have had a significant influence on changes in the number of visitors. They include large and small sites, high and low priced sites, sites with large price increases over the period and sites with small price increases. They include some sites where quite good explanations of visitor trends can be achieved through the use of other variables - but also some sites where very little statistical explanation could be achieved by use of any of the variables included in this analysis. For all of these sites, it may be assumed that visits have not been significantly affected by increases in admission prices. For some sites, of course, it is possible that more complex modelling of influences on visits might show up a price effect, but it is not likely that this could be large.

Table 8.22

Preferred estimates of price elasticity of demand for visits to sites derived from simple and multivariate regressions

(a) National Trust Sites

Site	Estimate of Price Elasticity
Chedworth	−0.36
Hardwick	—
Hidcote	−0.85 to −1.05
Knightshayes	—
Knole	—
Packwood	−0.8 to −1.0
St. Michael's Mount	—
Sheffield Park	−0.6 to −0.7
Shugborough	−0.35 to −0.5
Tatton Gardens	—
Tatton Hall	—
Waddesdon	—
Wallington	−0.25 to −0.3

(b) D.O.E. Sites

Site	Estimate of Price Elasticity
Audley End	—
Avebury	−0.15 to −0.20
Carisbrook	−0.33 to −0.30
Castle Acre	—
Chesters Roman Fort	—
Dover Castle	−0.20 to −0.30
Fountains	—
Framlingham	—
Goodrich	−0.2 to −0.35
Hampton Court	−0.2 to −0.3
Housesteads	—
Kenilworth	−0.5
Lindisfarne	—
Lullingstone	−0.13 to −0.5
Orford	—
Osborne	−0.55 to −0.70
Richmond	−0.25 to −0.30
Rievaulx	—
Scarborough	−0.25 to −0.36
Stonehenge	—
Walmer	−0.09 to −0.18
Whitby	—

9 Validation case studies

Introduction

In order to test the validity of the results obtained from the time series analysis, detailed case studies were carried out at six sites. The sites chosen (Audley End, Chedworth Roman Villa, Hidcote Manor Garden, Packwood House, Shugborough and Tatton Park) embrace a range of locations, sizes and facilities as well as a variety of charging structures. The detailed examination of variations in the number and distribution of visits to these properties, coupled with discussions with the site managers and administrators, highlighted some of the circumstances which are likely to modify price elasticity significantly and some of the practical constraints on the adoption of alternative charging strategies designed to achieve site management as well as financial goals.

Audley End

The property, comprising a Jacobean country house with eighteenth century additions set in 100 acres of grounds, is located one mile west of Saffron Walden in Essex. Facilities for visitors include a restaurant situated within the house, and a small agricultural museum and a nursery garden both of which were opened to the public in 1975.

The site, which is owned and administered by the Department of the Environment, is open from 10.00 a.m. to 5.30 p.m. Tuesday to Sunday between the months of April to October. An experiment involving an extension of the opening season was made in 1977 and 1978, but abandoned in 1979.

Charging system

A single charge is made for admission to the house and grounds from a ticket booth located just inside the main entrance. An additional charge for parking within the grounds was operated until May 1976, when it was removed as a result of protests from season ticket holders and problems caused by off-site parking.

Throughout the period studied, decisions on the level of admission charges were taken centrally by the DoE in London. Over this period the adult admission charge increased from 15 pence in 1971 to £1.50 in 1981. This represented a doubling of the admission price in real terms (Figure 9.1).

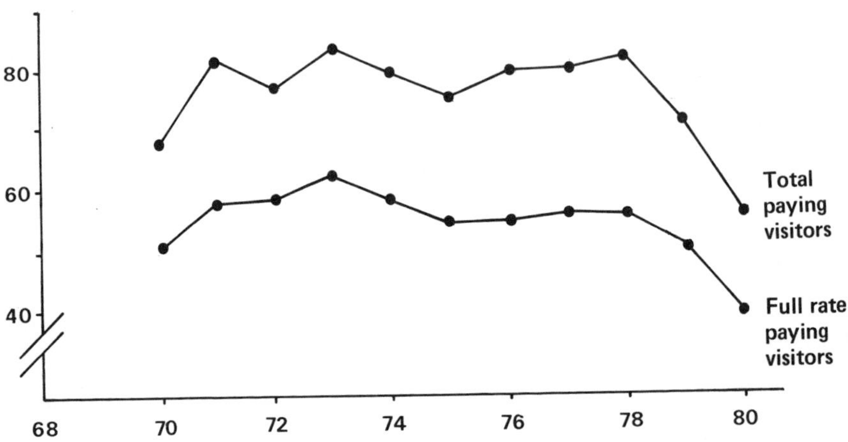

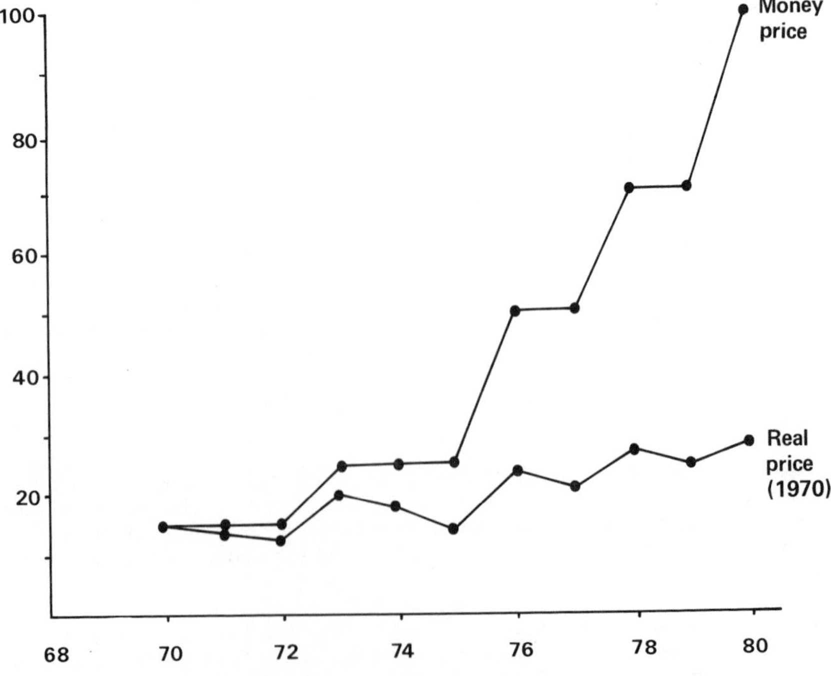

Figure 9.1 Change in admission prices and the number of paying visitors at Audley End

Trends in visitor numbers

The total number of visitors paying the full rate for admission fluctuated around 55-60,000 from 1971 until 1978. Since then the numbers have experienced a steep decline (Figure 9.1). Less marked falls in the number of paying visitors were experienced in 1974 and 1975 and a further fall of around 25% occurred in 1981. Over the period from 1978 to 1980 just over 27% of paying visits were made during the peak month of August and a further 15% during July (Figure 9.9(a)).

The influence of variations in admission prices

For most of the period studied there appears to have been little relationship between increases in admission charges and changes in the number of visitors. Thus, the number of paying visitors remained fairly constant in the period from 1975 to 1978, despite fairly substantial real increases in the admission charges (Figure 9.1). Not surprisingly, therefore, the initial analyses of monthly admissions data showed a very weak correlation between changes in admission charges and changes in the number of paying visitors.

A significant relationship was, however, found between the level of admission charges and the number of paying visitors. This implied an average drop of 31 visits per month for every penny increase in the admission charge in money terms and a fall of 130 visits for every penny increase in real terms. Moreover, there is some indication that consumer reaction to such increases was increasing towards the end of the period examined. Thus the 1980 increase from 70 to 100 pence was associated with a 22% decrease in the number of paying visitors and the 1981 increase from 100 to 150 pence was associated with a further decrease of around 25%. The site custodians certainly believe that this level of admission charges has been a substantial deterrent to visitors.

The influence of other variables

Over the period studied the two most significant influences on variations in the number of visitors from year to year seem to have been changes in petrol prices and changes in the level of average earnings and unemployment within the region (Tables 8.14 to 8.17). Whilst no formal visitor surveys have been conducted at the site, it is apparent that the majority of visits originate from more than 30 miles distance. It is perhaps not surprising, therefore, that increases in petrol prices appear to be significantly correlated with drops in the number of visits to the site. The steepest drops in numbers, in 1974-75 and 1979-80, coincided with sharp increases in the price of petrol and oil (Figure 9.2). A particular decline in the number of visits from organised coach tours has been noticed by the site custodians. However, a more significant factor underlying the decline in the number of visitors after 1979 has been the opening of the M11, which has drastically reduced the amount of traffic which previously passed the main entrance to the site.

When account is taken of these factors, the influence of changes in admission prices is enhanced appreciably - particularly if the last few years of the study period are considered in isolation. It is, however, difficult to separate their specific influence from other factors which have also changed during this period.

(a) RPI

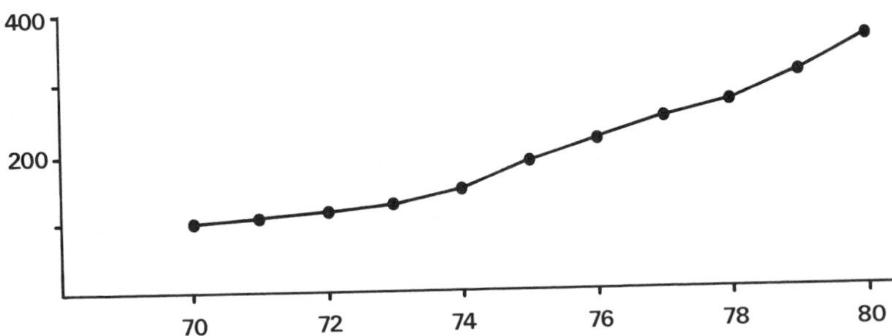

(b) Petrol/oil prices

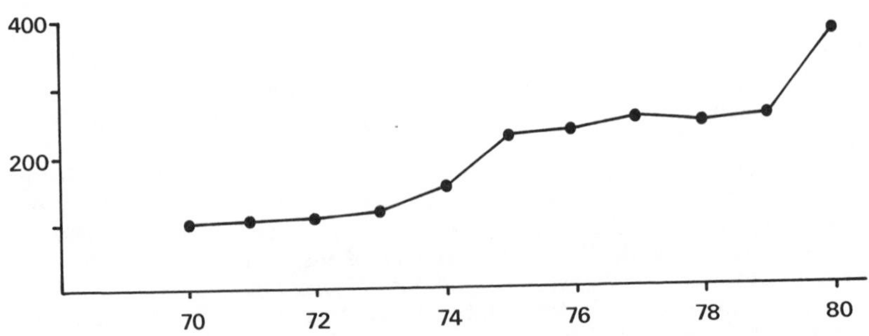

Figure 9.2 **Change in Retail Prices Index and petrol prices 1970-80**

Promotion and advertising

During the study period virtually all promotion and advertising for this site was arranged by the DoE's Ancient Monuments and Historic Buildings Division at Saville Row, London. This included a listing in the publication 'Historic Houses and Gardens Open to the Public'. The house was also featured, along with others in the region, in a leaflet which was distributed free of charge and on leaflets promoting season tickets.

Promotion at the local level has been confined to the circulation of leaflets to the Regional Tourist Board's information centres, coach and tour operators, and to groups which have visited the property on previous occasions. The property has also been featured fairly frequently in the local press and was used as a 'back-cloth' for photography for a mail order catalogue in 1980.

In recent years the grounds have also been used for a number of small scale local events. These have included a 'May Ball', and a special event held in aid of Saffron Walden church. However, since these were generally held after normal opening times, they appear to have had no detectable effect on the number of paying visitors. They may, however, have increased people's awareness of the property.

Other events, such as veteran car rallies, held in June 1976, 1977 and 1978, seem to have been associated with slight increases in the number of paying visitors in this month. However, in 1978 it is difficult to separate this effect from the influence of publicity received in one of the Sunday newspaper colour supplements; the May Day Bank Holiday and the general increase in visitors associated with the Queen's Silver Jubilee celebrations. Admissions also tend to benefit to some extent from other events held in the vicinity, such as a special event at a nearby miniature railway. In contrast, occasional features on local television, such as in July 1978 and April 1981, are considered by the site custodians to have had a marked temporary effect on the number of visits.

Chedworth Roman Villa

The site, which is owned and administered by the National Trust, comprises the remains of a Romano - British villa, set in six and a half acres of woodland at Yanworth, eight miles north of Cirencester in Gloucestershire. Until 1978 the main features of the site comprised well preserved mosaic pavements, a bath house and a museum which houses some of the smaller objects discovered during excavations. In December 1978 these attractions were enhanced by the opening of a new visitors' reception area incorporating a display of interpretative material and a National Trust shop. Nine months later the interpretative facilities were further enhanced by the opening of a small lecture theatre with audio-visual display facilities - including an automatic tape-slide commentary highlighting the main stages of the site's development. With the incorporation of these new facilities opening hours were extended from 11.00 a.m. until 6.00 p.m. in summer and until 4.00 p.m. in winter.

Charging system

A single scale of charges for admission to the site is operated throughout the year with no winter reduction. Prices are determined at the regional level by a committee in the light of guidance issued by the Trust's head office staff. Specific recommendations are intended to take account of any enhancement to facilities which has taken place as well as the reaction of visitors to previous price increases. Account is also taken of charges made at comparable properties operated by the private sector. No charge is made for car parking.

Apart from a fairly substantial increase in 1973, admission prices were maintained at a fairly constant level in real terms until 1978. Since then, they have been increased substantially in both money and real terms (Figure 9.3). This reflects a conscious effort by the Trust to achieve a return on the capital invested in the new facilities provided at the site.

Trends in visitor numbers

The total number of paying visitors to the site increased fairly steadily from around 60,000 in 1968 to around 68,000 in 1973. The sharp fall in the following year was followed by a stabilisation and slow recovery to around 66,000 visits in 1977. Thereafter, the number of paying visitors dropped steeply to around 49,000 in 1980. Over this period the number of visits made by National Trust members increased fairly steadily and by 1980 these accounted for around 28% of the total number of visitors.

During the period from 1978 to 1980 the total number of visitors in each week generally climbed fairly steadily from around 6-700 per week in early March to a peak of around 3,500 - 4,500 around the August Bank Holiday period. Thereafter, numbers tended to decline fairly rapidly to around 2,000 per week by the end of September. Substantial peaks were also associated with the Easter and Spring Bank Holidays. Just over 17% of paying visits were made during the peak month of August (Figure 9.9(b)).

Until 1981 car parking facilities were very limited with resultant problems of congestion at peak visiting times. In July of that year, however, a new car parking area with picnic facilities was opened within an area of woodland a few hundred yards from the visitor reception area. This is intended to intercept some of the visitors who would otherwise have parked closer to the villa itself.

Visitor surveys carried out in 1978 and 1979 indicated that between 75 and 80% of all visitors were visiting Chedworth for the first time. School children comprise a substantial proportion of visitors to the site during weekdays and, since most schools make advance bookings for such visits, it is possible for the custodians to even out the pressure placed on the site's facilities by such groups.

The influence of variations in admission prices

Falls in the total number of paying visitors coincided with increases in admission charges in 1970 and in each of the years from 1977 to 1980 (Figure 9.3). The 1973 increase also appears to have had a lagged effect on the number of paying visitors in 1974. In 1975 and 1976, however, the numbers of paying visitors increased slightly despite increases in admission prices.

This apparent negative correlation between changes in admission prices and

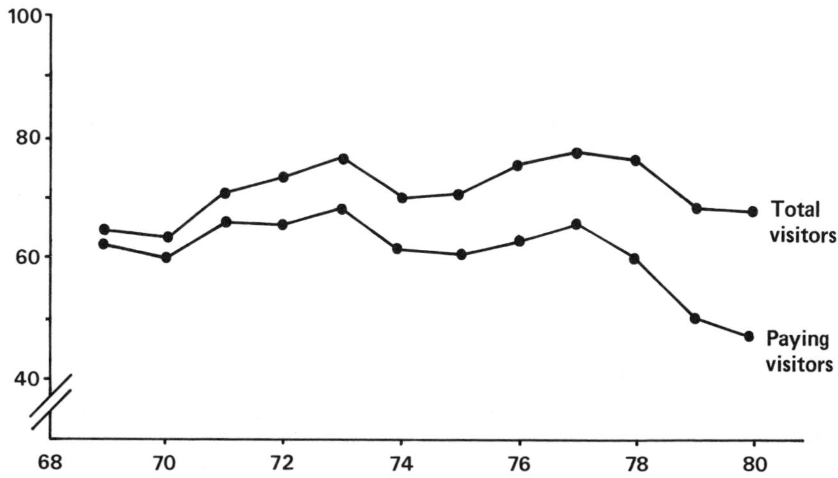

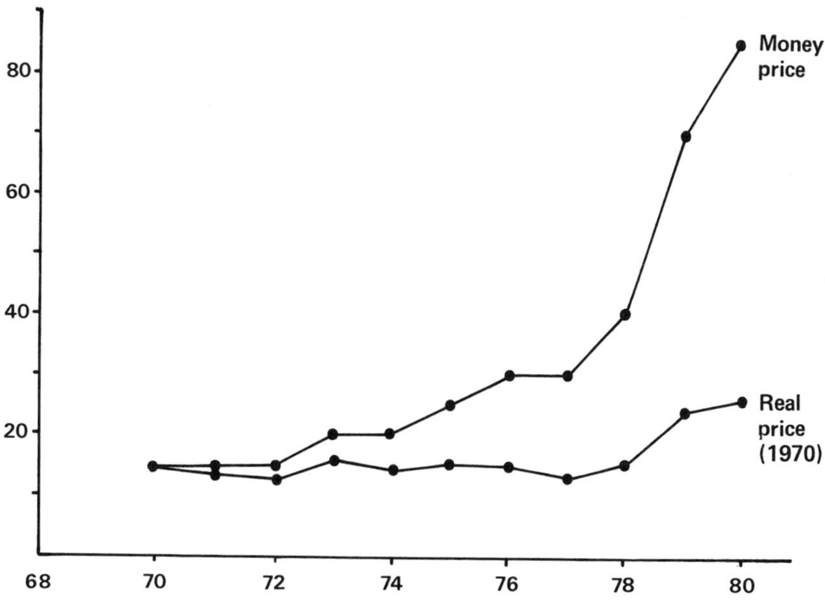

Figure 9.3 Changes in admission prices and number of paying visitors at Chedworth

changes in the number of paying visitors is also reflected in the monthly data. Taking the period from 1974-80 as a whole, significant correlations were found between the level of both real and money admission charges and changes in the number of visitors (Tables 8.8, 8.11 and 8.13). These results imply a drop of 50-60 visitors a month for every penny increase in the admission charge and a drop of 170-229 for every penny increase in real terms. This in turn implies an elasticity value of around -0.36.

The 1981 increase in the adult admission price from £0.85 to £1.20 was particularly steep in percentage terms and this price level was felt by both the site custodian and the regional administrators to have been a substantial deterrent to visitors. During the spring of 1981 a check on the number of people turning away after reading the scale of admission charges was maintained. This suggested an average 'turn-around' of 20-25%, with a figure as high as 40% on some days. At weekends, however, the proportion generally dropped to 11-13%. In the light of this apparent reaction, the admission price was pegged at £1.20 during 1982.

The influence of other factors

Not surprisingly, given the relatively open nature of the site, the most significant influence on changes in the number of visits to Chedworth, apart from the admission price, appears to be the weather. In particular, the number of visits in any particular month tends to drop fairly substantially with an increase in the number of rain days (Tables 8.10 to 8.13). None of the other variables tested in the analysis - including indices of changes in petrol prices and the running costs of private vehicles - appear to relate consistently to changes in the number of visits. However, increases in petrol prices were considered by the site custodian to have had an influence, and the fall in the number of visits from 1973-75 did in fact take place against a background of steep increases in petrol prices.

The opening of the new visitor centre seems to have been associated with an increase in the number of National Trust members visiting the site, but has had no detectable positive influence on the number of paying visitors. In part, of course, this may reflect the more effective marketing of membership which has been made possible by the construction of the new reception area. This, along with the narrowing differential between membership fees and the admission charges noted in Chapter 8, seems likely to have encouraged an increasing proportion of casual visitors to opt for membership rather than pay the admission charge.

Whilst neither the new commercial facilities nor the audio-visual display appear to have had any significant effect on the number of paying visitors, the site custodian believes that visitors do go away from the site better informed and more satisfied.

Promotion and advertising

All promotion of the site is handled by the Trust's regional office rather than the custodian. In the mid to late 1970's it was considered that the site was suffering from excessive pressure from visitors at peak periods. Consequently, promotional efforts have been limited. Publicity material comprises a property leaflet which is distributed through a variety of outlets such as tourist information centres, public libraries, museums etc., as well as an inclusion on a display card featuring several properties in the region which is designed for hotel notice boards. New style National Trust signs to the site were erected on the adjacent main roads in 1980.

The direct effects of this promotion on visits seems, however, to have been fairly limited. Thus, visitor surveys conducted in 1978 and 1979 indicated that around a third of all visitors came to the site after learning about it from friends or relatives and around 40% became aware of it from the National Trust's guide to 'Properties Open to the Public'. Far smaller proportions visited the site as a result of seeing information on hotel notice boards (7%); library information boards (3%); or from seeing an individual property leaflet (3%). A substantial proportion of casual visitors also came to the site after learning about it from the Corinium Museum in Cirencester. School parties also frequently combine visits to these two sites.

Given the restricted nature of the site and the vulnerability of its main features, very few special events have been staged. A display by the 'Ermine Street Guard' in July 1978 received very little advance publicity and did not appear to enhance the number of visitors to the site. Since the opening of the shop, however, advertisements have also been placed in the local press at Christmas time and for special sales. These are believed to have had a slight, but noticeable, effect on the number of visitors at this time of year.

Hidcote Manor Garden

The site, which is owned and administered by the National Trust, comprises approximately ten acres of formal gardens in the small hamlet of Hidcote Bartrim, four miles north-east of Chipping Camden in Gloucestershire. The gardens, which are open five days a week from April to October, were created by the famous horticulturist Major Lawrence Johnston and are notable for their rare shrubs, trees and herbaceous borders. Facilities for visitors include a tea room and a National Trust shop.

Charging system

A single scale of admission charges is operated throughout the season. Visitors enter the site via a hallway adjacent to the shop and are guided back through the shop on their return. Parking for coaches and private vehicles is provided free of charge a short distance away.

A peak pricing system was considered by the regional administrators during the mid seventies as a possible solution to the serious problems caused by the large number of visitors attracted to the site at certain weekends during the season. However, the scheme was rejected on the grounds that it would be too complicated to administer and instead a series of substantial across the board increases were introduced. The increase in the adult admission charge from 30 pence in 1974 to £1.10 in 1980 represented a 52% increase in real terms (Figure 9.4).

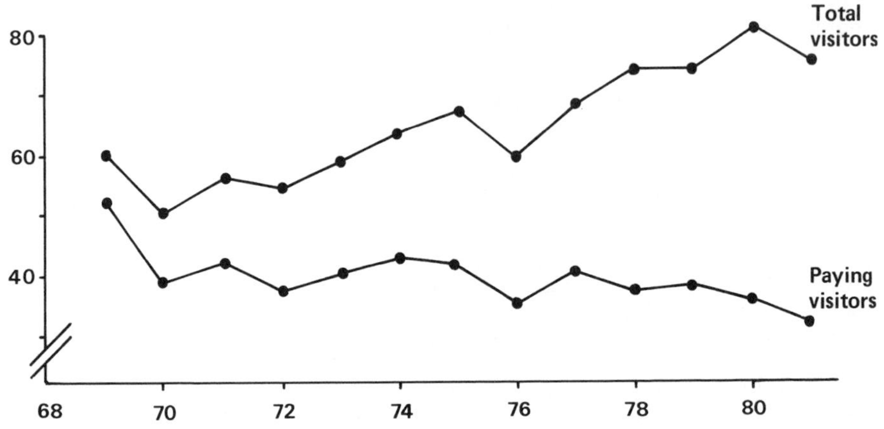

(b) Adult admission price (pence)

100
80
60
40
20
Money price
Real price (1970)
68
70
72
74
76
78
80

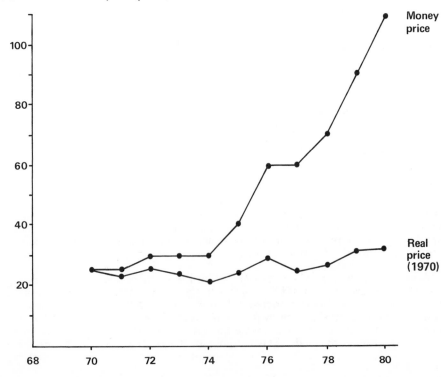

Figure 9.4 Changes in admission prices and number of paying visitors at Hidcote Manor Garden

Trends in visitor numbers

The total number of visitors to the site grew fairly steadily from around 50,000 in 1968 to more than 81,000 in 1980. Above average increases in the number of visitors occurred in 1969 and 1971, and a substantial fall in the number of visitors occurred in 1976 (Figure 9.4). In contrast, the total number of paying visitors reached a peak of 53,000 in 1969, dropped to 40,000 in the subsequent year and fluctuated around this level until 1977, since when numbers have declined fairly steadily. The gap between the two totals is, of course, explained by a substantial growth in the number of visits to the site by National Trust members (Figure 9.4).

Over the period from 1978 to 1980 just under 23% of paying visits were made during the peak month of July and a further 19% during August. In contrast, visits by members were generally more evenly distributed throughout the opening season (Figure 9.9(c)).

The influence of variations in admission prices

Over the period from 1974 to 1980 year-on-year variations in the number of paying visitors to the site showed significant negative correlations with variations in price. The analysis which was carried out on changes in the number of visits in each month during this period implies a fall of around 60 paying visitors per month for every penny increase in money prices, and a fall of 181 paying visitors for every penny increase in real prices. This implies an elasticity value of around -0.85 for money prices and around -1.00 for real prices.

As is the case of Chedworth and other National Trust properties, the decrease in the ratio of the membership fee to the admission charge seems to have encouraged a significant proportion of casual visitors to opt for membership of the Trust as a means of gaining access to the site (Table 8.20). The regional administrators also consider that the increases in admission prices have brought about a better distribution of visits over the week.

The influence of other factors

Given the open nature of the site and the nature of its main attractions we would expect weather to exert a significant influence on the number of visits. The prolonged drought in 1976 and the late spring in 1981 are therefore felt by the site managers to have been a significant factor in the decline in the number of visits in these two years. However, neither changes in the number of rain days nor the amount of sunshine appeared as significant variables in the analysis of year-on-year changes of monthly visits over the study period as a whole.

The weak negative correlation between changes in the number of paying visitors and changes in the real running costs of private cars suggests that increases in travel costs have tended to depress visits to the site. However, the fact that the fall-off in the number of paying visitors from 1974 to 1976 and 1979 to 1981 coincided with an increase in both admission prices and petrol costs means that it is very difficult to distinguish the separate effects of these two trends. Consequently, changes in petrol prices appear, rather perversely, to show a positive correlation with changes in the number of visits. When account was taken of such factors in the analysis, however, the significance of increases in admission prices was generally enhanced and the elasticity values increased to around -0.96 to -1.00 for both real and money prices.

The changes which can be expected to occur in the appearance of the gardens with the seasons are probably an important factor in encouraging visitors to make repeat visits. Visitor surveys carried out in 1977 and 1978 indicated that more than 40% of visitors had visited the site before. The tearooms at Hidcote are also felt to be an important factor in encouraging National Trust members to make further visits.

Promotion and advertising

Along with other properties in the region the site is featured in the Trust's regional guides and in a pamphlet detailing properties within 60 miles of Birmingham. Both these leaflets are distributed free of charge via the Heart of England Tourist Board and direct to information points, libraries, hotels etc. in the major towns within the region. Hidcote was also included in advertisements which the Trust placed in the local press, such as the Coventry Evening Telegraph, Sutton Coldfield News and Sunday Mercury, whose circulation centres on the West Midlands conurbation. These advertisements, which have generally appeared during the early part of the summer season from mid-May to early June, have probably increased the general level of awareness of the property, but there was no apparent correlation between the timing of these and changes in the number of visitors to Hidcote.

Since 1977, performances of open-air plays have been staged in the gardens during July. These events have proved extremely popular and advertisements for them in the local press and magazines may again have increased awareness of the property. However, since performances take place in the evenings, when the site is normally closed to the public, it was not possible to detect any direct influence on the number of paying visitors to the site. The regional administrators do, however, consider that these are responsible for bringing people back to the gardens for visits on future occasions. The total number of visits to the site during July and August have certainly shown a tendency to increase in recent years. The use of the gardens as the setting for a BBC television programme broadcast in June 1980 may also be partially responsible for the increase in the number of visits in this month.

Packwood House

This property is located approximately eleven miles south-east of central Birmingham, some two miles from the main road to Stratford-upon-Avon (A34). The property, which is administered by the National Trust, comprises a 16th century house and gardens set amongst 113 acres of park and woodland. The main features of the house include a collection of tapestry and furniture, whilst the gardens include a Carolean formal garden and a notable yew garden containing fine examples of topiary.

In terms of both the size of the property and the visitor numbers, this was by far the smallest of the sites studied in detail - attracting only 26,000 visitors in

1980. During the study period the house was open all the year round, but days and times of opening were restricted between October and the end of March.

Charging system

Separate charges are made for visitors wishing to view the house and gardens or the gardens only. Tickets are sold from a small desk located in the entrance hallway to the house. The full adult admission charge was increased steadily from 20 pence in 1972 to 85 pence in 1980. In real terms, however, it has remained relatively stable - fluctuating between 21 and 25 pence in terms of 1970 prices (Figure 9.5).

Trends in visitor numbers

The total number of visitors to the property reached a peak of 26,000 in 1971 and experienced a steady decline until 1976, since when visits have increased gradually. This recovery has, however, been largely due to an appreciable increase in the number of visits by National Trust members and, with few exceptions, the number of paying visitors attracted to the site each year has shown a steady decline since 1971 (Figure 9.5).

Over the period from 1978 to 1980 just under a third of all paying visits were made during the peak months of July and August (Figure 9.9(d)). Just over 29% of visits by members of the Trust were also made during these two months.

The influence of variations in admission prices

In the period studied, changes in the level of admission charges and changes in the number of paying visitors were very closely correlated. Thus, analysis of year-on-year changes in the number of paying visitors admitted in each month over the 1973-80 period showed a significant negative correlation with changes in both real and money admission prices (Tables 8.6 and 8.8). The equations derived from these analyses imply an elasticity value of -0.8 to -1.0 (Table 8.21).

The influence of other variables

The time series analysis summarised in Chapter 8 identified a significant positive time-trend and some indication that the number of visits is sensitive to variations in the weather and changes in the running costs of private cars (Table 8.13). When account is taken of such factors, however, the elasticity values remain virtually unchanged and in the range -0.9 to -1.0.

A substantial growth in the number and proportion of visits by members of the Trust has taken place in recent years, rising from 4,869 (21%) in 1974 to 11,679 (45%) in 1980. This feature, however, seems to reflect the growth in membership of the Trust and there is little evidence that the level of admission charges over this period has acted as an inducement for a significant proportion of casual visitors to opt for membership rather than pay the admission charge.

(a) Visitors (000)

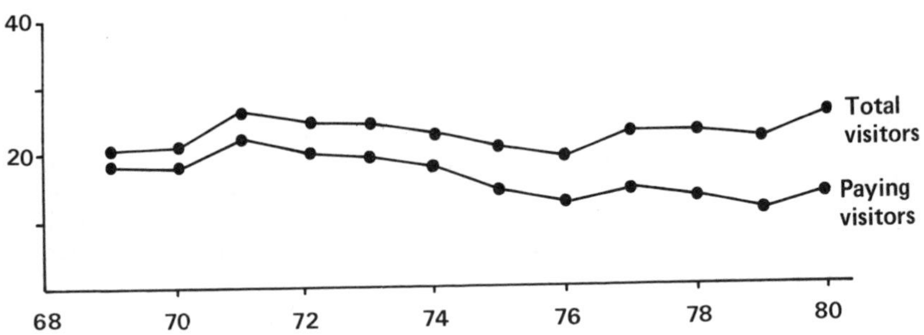

(b) Adult admission price (pence)

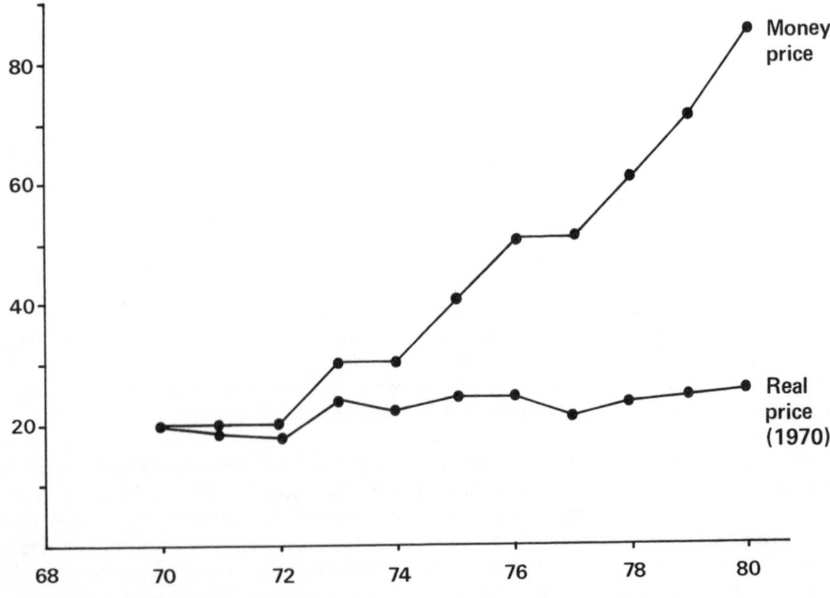

Figure 9.5 Changes in admission prices and number of paying visitors at Packwood House

Advertising and promotion

The terms of the covenant under which the property was given to the Trust tends to restrict the manner in which the house can be presented to the public, and this constrains the extent to which it is possible to promote it in order to attract a greater number of visitors. However, Packwood was amongst a number of properties in the Severn Region for which special efforts were made during 1981 to increase visitors. The property was featured in advertisements placed in the Coventry Evening Telegraph, Sutton Coldfield News and Sunday Mercury in May, June and August and also appeared on the front page of the 1981 version of the Severn Region's guide to properties open to the public. The property is also included in the Trust's guide to properties within 60 miles of Birmingham. Both these leaflets are available free of charge at tourist information centres, public libraries etc.

Despite this promotional effort, the number of paying visitors actually declined by around 18% during 1981 compared with the previous year. This decrease was, however, substantially less than decreases which occurred at properties such as Chedworth and Charlecote Park where no particular promotional efforts were made.

Shugborough

This site lies roughly six miles east of Stafford, adjacent to Cannock Chase, and comprises an imposing late 17th century country house set in an extensive park which contains neoclassical monuments, follies, riverside terraces and rose gardens. The property is owned by the National Trust, but the house and parts of the grounds are leased and administered by Staffordshire County Council.

The restored coach-houses, brewhouse, and laundry form part of the Staffordshire County Museum, and contain reconstructed shops, a school room and displays of domestic life, toys, costumes and crafts. Other facilities within this complex include a National Trust shop as well as a cafe and a separate souvenir shop operated by Staffordshire County Council. A Georgian farmstead within the park has displays of farm machinery and rare local breeds of livestock. During the study period the house was open from 10.30 to 5.30 p.m. Tuesdays to Fridays and from 2.00 to 5.30 p.m. at weekends during the period from late March until the end of October. The museum and farmstead were also open during the winter months.

Charging system

The structure and level of charges and the system adopted for making these varied appreciably during the study period. Until 1979, admission to the grounds and museum was free and the only charges made were for parking vehicles and for admission to the house itself. During 1978 and 1979 the charge for parking was only operated at weekends. However, in view of problems caused by off-site parking, this system was replaced in 1979 by a system involving separate charges for admission to the grounds and the house and no additional charge for parking. Until 1980 a 50% discount on admission charges was available for parties of 20 or more.

There are two public access points to the site - one for vehicles via the main entrance at Milford on the A513 Stafford to Lichfield road, and one, for pedestrians only, via a footbridge which connects the site to the nearby village of Great Haywood. The range of options on when and where to charge admission fees is constrained to some extent by the presence of the public footbridge from Great Haywood, and by the fire brigade's insistence on the operation of a one-way traffic system within the grounds. Ticket booths are currently located at the entrance to the car park, inside the main entrance to the house itself and at the entrance to the gardens adjacent to the footbridge from Great Haywood.

Increases in admission prices which have been introduced in recent years have been aimed at producing a progressive reduction in the site's operating deficit. The increase in the charge for admission to the house from 10 pence in 1971 to 60 pence in 1979 represented a 100% increase in real terms (Figure 9.6). In the subsequent year the admission price was reduced by 10 pence.

Trends in visitor numbers

With the exception of a slight decline in 1972, the total number of visitors to the house increased fairly steadily in each year from around 20,000 in 1968 to around 46,000 in 1974 (Figure 9.6). In subsequent years the total number of visitors declined sharply to around 30,000 in 1975; recovered to around 35,000 in 1976 and since then has fluctuated around this level. The total number of paying visitors also followed a rising trend from 1968 until 1974, but since then has experienced a substantial and progressive decline (Figure 9.6).

No formal visitor surveys have been undertaken at the site. However, the site administrators consider that the bulk of visitors during the week comprise parties and retired couples; the majority of those visiting on Sundays tend to be 'day-trippers', and the bulk of those visiting on Saturdays are National Trust Members. Parties of pensioners tend to visit the site at times when school parties do not - i.e. during school holidays and during afternoons rather than mornings.

Visits by National Trust members accounted for a very small proportion of total visits up until 1976. Since then, however, the proportion has increased substantially to reach around 35% by 1980. Over the period from 1978 to 1980 just over 26% of all paying visits were made during the peak month of August and a further 16% during July (Figure 9.9(e)). The corresponding proportions for visits by members of the National Trust were 22% and 16%.

The large number of visitors attracted to the site at peak hours during Bank Holidays and at weekends has placed considerable strains on amenities such as the cafe and toilets. The car park charge, operated at weekends during 1978 and 1979, was in part introduced in an attempt to spread this load. However, in addition to the problems arising from off-site parking by visitors seeking to avoid the charge, this proved cumbersome to administer.

The influence of variations in admission prices

The pattern of change in the number of paying visitors over the study period as a whole appears to have been closely correlated with changes in admission

(a) Visitors (000)

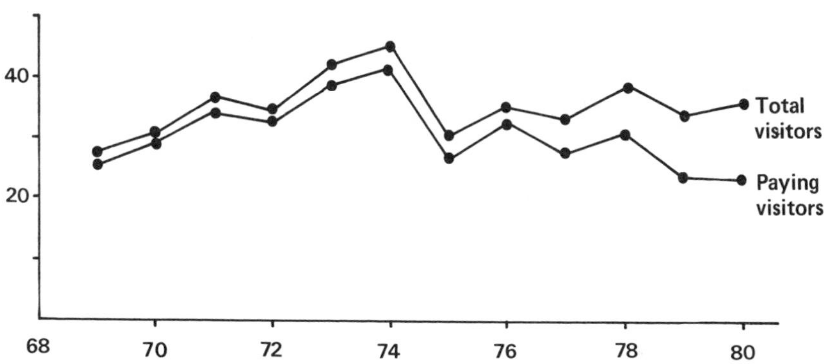

(b) Adult admission price (pence)

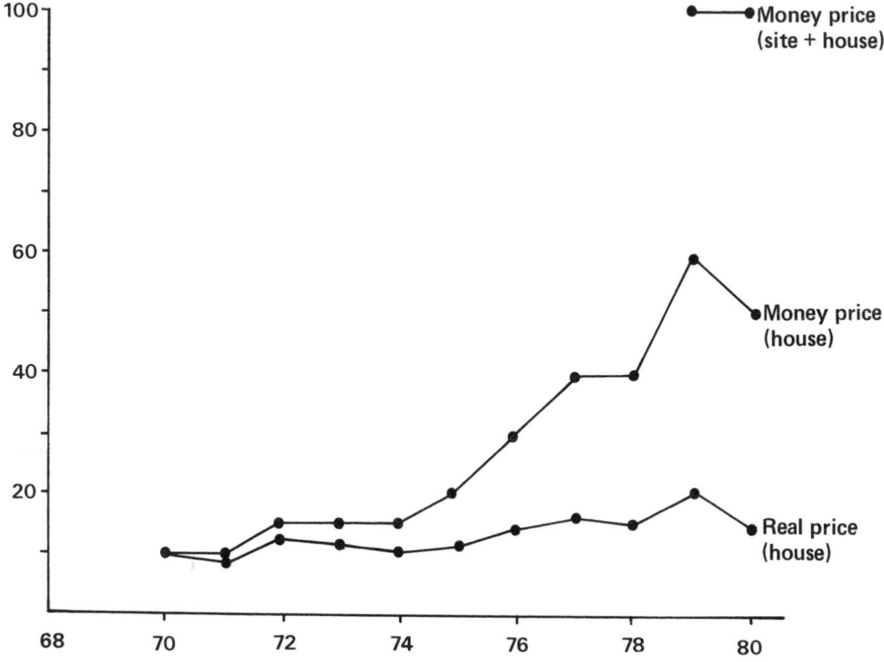

Figure 9.6 **Changes in admission prices and number of paying visitors at Shugborough**

prices. Thus, falls in the total number of paying visitors coincided with increases in prices in 1972, 1975, 1977 and 1979. This correlation was confirmed by the analysis of monthly data. Over the period from 1973 to 1980, therefore, year-on-year changes in the number of paying visitors admitted in each month showed a significant correlation with changes in both money and real prices (Tables 8.6 and 8.8). The regression coefficients in these correlations imply an elasticity value of around -0.3 for changes in money prices and a slightly higher value for changes in real prices. These values are very close to the assumptions which the administrators have recently incorporated into the financial planning for the site.

Charges for admission to the house over most of this period have been fixed at levels which are substantially less than those at comparable sites administered directly by the National Trust. It is not surprising, therefore, that there appears to have been no significant tendency for paying visitors to this site to opt for membership of the Trust rather than pay the admission charge. The numbers visiting the house as members of parties booked in advance have, however, dropped off very substantially since the concessionary rate was abandoned in 1980.

Changes in the charging system have also had a variety of side-effects. Thus, the site administrators consider that the introduction of a site charge, whilst expensive to administer - in view of the need to staff two access points as well as the entrance to the house itself - has had the effect of reducing the incidence of petty vandalism.

The influence of other factors

The analysis of monthly data suggested that the most significant influences on visits over the 1973 to 1980 period, apart from changes in admission prices, were changes in the costs of private transport and variations in the weather from year to year. The influence of these factors is indicated by the significant correlations between changes in the running costs of private cars, petrol prices and the number of rain days and changes in the number of paying visitors during this period (Tables 8.10 to 8.13). Again, these inferences, based on the statistical evidence, accord closely with the subjective perceptions of the site administrators. The fall in the number of visitors in 1975, for example, coincided with a steep increase in petrol prices (Figure 9.2). However, this correlation is less evident in later years. For some reason which is not apparent, however, paying visits to this site seem to show a significant positive correlation with changes in the level of unemployment within the West Midlands region.

Advertising and promotion

The budget available for publicising this property has been extremely small (£900 in 1981/2). This has been used mainly to cover the production of free leaflets distributed to the public via information centres and hotels. Competition from other sites within the region - particularly those, such as Alton Towers and Weston Park, which have undertaken extensive promotional and marketing campaigns - is considered to have been a significant factor underlying the fall off in the number of paying visitors in recent years.

The size and layout of the land leased by the County Council does not lend itself to the staging of large scale outdoor events in the vicinity of the house itself. A number of small scale events, including folk dancing displays and veteran car club rallies, were held on the site during the study period. Generally, however, these received very little advance publicity and thus, not surprisingly, it was not possible to detect any significant influence on the number of paying visitors to the site. As in the case of Tatton Hall, the site administrators are conscious that the house itself tends to be a 'static' display. Change within the site is, however, regarded as vital in encouraging people to make repeat visits. The need for this has underlain the move to develop additional facilities within the site, such as the farm and a display of the County's historic vehicles collection.

Tatton Park

The park is located two miles north of Knutsford and thirteen miles south-west of Manchester, close to the M6 and M56 motorways. The property comprises an 18th century house set in 50 acres of landscaped formal gardens and surrounded by more than 1,000 acres of deer park. A large lake within the park, known as Tatton Mere, supports many varieties of wildfowl. The estate is owned by the National Trust, but is leased and administered by Cheshire County Council. In terms of both area and number of visitors this was the largest of the sites studied in detail. It is estimated that just under 500,000 people visit the park each year. During 1980 the house attracted 132,000 visitors and the gardens 177,000.

Facilities associated with the house include a museum, audio-visual display, restaurant and National Trust shop - opened in 1977. Features within the park include a medieval manor house (Tatton Old Hall) which was opened to the public in 1980 and a deserted medieval village interpretation 'trail'. Facilities for active water-based recreation such as wind-surfing, sailing and fishing are available at Tatton Mere.

The park and garden are open to the public throughout the year. The house, however, is closed from October to April. Precise opening times vary appreciably throughout the year. In particular, public access to the house and gardens is extended to seven days a week during August and confined to Sundays during the early and later parts of the year.

Charging system

Separate charges are made for admission to the house, gardens and the Old Hall. In addition a charge is made for all vehicles entering the park and for vehicles using a car park provided at the Knutsford Gate entrance (70 pence for cars in 1981). Pedestrians are admitted to the park free of charge.

The level of admission charges is determined by a management committee in the light of advice from the County Treasurer. Admission charges for both house and gardens were increased steadily in both money and real terms from 1974 until 1978 (Figures 9.7 and 9.8). Since then the level of charges has fallen slightly in real terms. As a result, admission prices have tended to be rather lower than those charged for comparable properties administered directly by

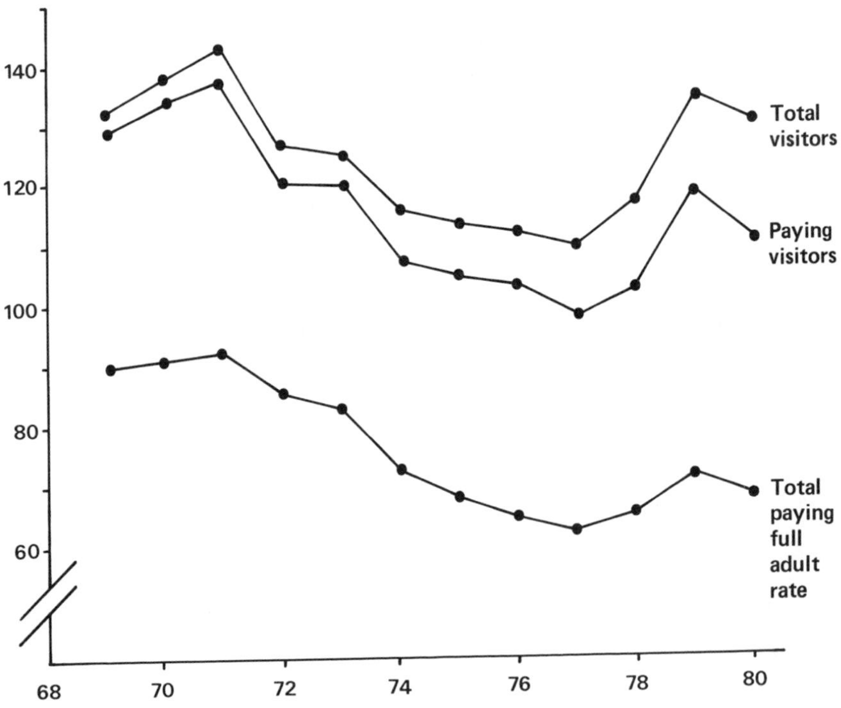

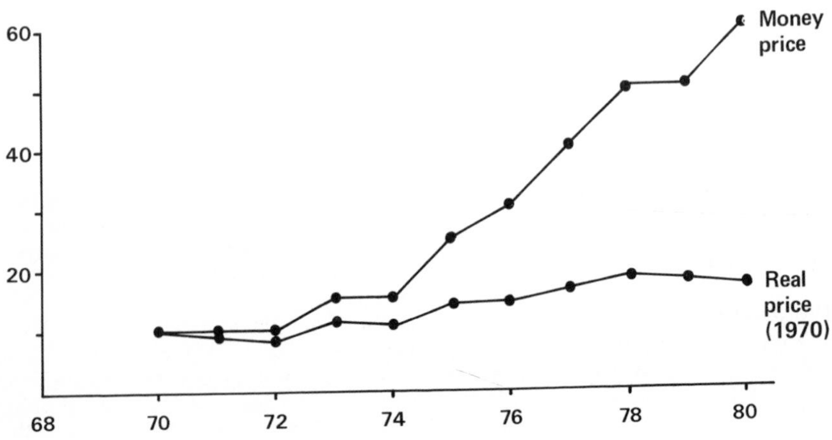

Figure 9.7 **Changes in admission prices and number of visitors at Tatton Hall**

(a) Visitors (000)

180
160
140
120
100
80

Total visitors

Total paying full adult rate

68 70 72 74 76 78 80

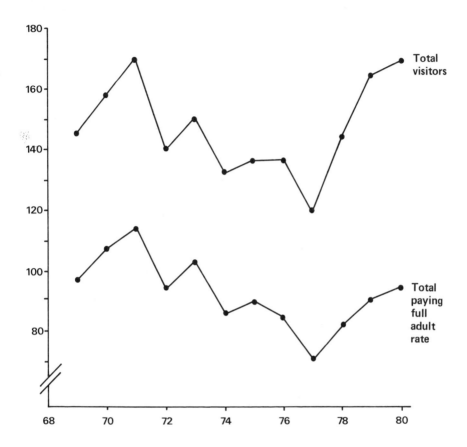

(b) Adult admission price (pence)

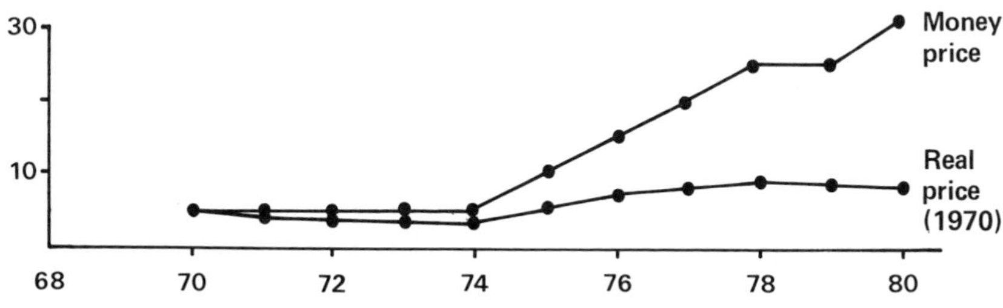

Figure 9.8 **Changes in admission prices and number of visitors at Tatton Gardens**

the National Trust. The current policy is, however, to increase charges in line with or slightly faster than the rate of inflation.

The range of concessionary rates offered was rationalised during 1981. Reduced rates are, however, available Tuesday to Saturday for parties of 15 or more booking in advance. During special events, such as the Cheshire Show or the Tatton Weekend Event, special admission charges are applied to all visitors entering the Park.

Trends in visitor numbers

The total number of visitors to both the house and the gardens reached a peak in 1971 and then declined sharply. This downward trend continued until 1977, when numbers began to rise once more (Figure 9.7). The number of paying visitors showed a very similar trend. The number of visitors to the gardens has, however, tended to fluctuate more from year to year - due mainly to variations in the weather (Figure 9.8). Taking the year as a whole, more than 40% of visits tend to occur on Sundays. Over the period from 1978 to 1980 just over 46% of all paying visits to the house and 45% of paying visits to the gardens were made during the peak months of July and August (Figure 9.9). The number of visits by members of the National Trust, whilst accounting for a relatively small proportion of the total compared with many sites, has shown a significant tendency to increase in recent years. Members' visits were rather more evenly distributed throughout the year, with 39% of visits to the house and 37% of visits to the gardens occurring during the peak months of July and August (Figure 9.9(f) and (g)).

A survey carried out in 1978 indicated that more than 86% of visitors came from within a 25 miles radius. The greatest concentration of visitors (50%) came from the Greater Manchester area, and particularly from Trafford, Stockport and Manchester Districts. A further 28% came from within Cheshire, and 72% of these came from the surrounding Districts of Warrington, Vale Royal and Macclesfield. The survey also indicated that more than 90% of visitors travelled to the site by private car. The fact that 46% of visitors had visited Tatton Park three or more times previously suggests that the recreational opportunities are varied enough to encourage repeat visits.

Comparison with national statistics shows that Tatton Park has tended to attract a high proportion of visitors in social classes I to III. Social class also appears to have had a noticeable effect on the frequency of visits - the trend being for those in higher social classes to make the greatest number of visits.

The influence of variations in admission prices

Whilst the number of paying visitors has tended to fall as admission charges have risen, the simple regression analysis failed to identify any significant correlation between year-on-year changes in admission prices and corresponding changes in the number of paying visitors (Tables 8.6 and 8.8). In the case of the gardens in fact, there has tended to be a positive relationship between changes in admission prices and changes in the number of paying visitors. The 1978 visitor survey indicated that the majority of visitors found the admission prices acceptable - and this tends to be substantiated by the high number of repeat visits. Nevertheless, approximately 17-18% of those interviewed in 1978 considered admission charges too high and there was also some indication that a proportion of visitors objected to being 'charged twice'.

The influence of other variables

Unfortunately, very few of the statistical models tested on monthly data provided significant explanations of variations in the number of paying visitors to either the house or the gardens. Changes in the number of visits to each of these facilities do, however, seem to have been influenced by rather different factors. Not surprisingly, the analysis indicated that the most significant influences on changes in the number of paying visits to the gardens over the period from 1974 to 1980 were variations in the weather. In particular, the number of paying visitors showed a tendency to increase with the amount of sunshine (Table 8.11) and, taking this period as a whole, the peak in the number of visits tended to occur between July and August. The peak in the number of paying visitors to the house, on the other hand tended to occur in August of each year. Visits to the house have shown a slight tendency to decline as levels of unemployment within the region have risen (Table 8.19).

Even when account was taken of such additional factors, however, no significant correlations were found between changes in admission prices and changes in the number of paying visitors. A possible explanation of the apparent insignificance of price increases has been the fact that admission prices have been increased by relatively small amounts each year. In consequence, they do not appear to have prompted any significant consumer resistance. The site custodians believe, however, that during 1981 the proportion of people turning away from the house after reading the price schedule rose from around 10-15% to around 20-30% following an increase in admission price from 60 pence to 70 pence coupled with a sharp rise in the charge for vehicles entering the Park.

The opening of the Old Hall is also believed to be a factor in the fall in the number of visitors to the house since 1980. Moreover, the site custodians consider that, since the house tends to be seen as a relatively 'static' display, it is far less effective in encouraging visitors to make repeat visits than the park or the gardens, which offer a wider range of recreational opportunities and change their appearance throughout the season. This belief seems to be borne out by the 1978 visitor survey which indicated that the gardens and the parkland were the features which frequent visitors to the site found most attractive. The Mere was also found to be particularly popular with frequent visitors.

Advertising and promotion

The budget available for promoting this property was larger than any of the other sites examined in detail. Promotion in recent years has included the production of posters and leaflets which are distributed free of charge, as well as advertisements in local newspapers and magazines, and television commercials. A wide range of events and functions are also held within the park each year. These include large scale annual events such as the Cheshire Show and Tatton Weekend Event, as well as smaller scale events which have included a Sealed Knot display, American Civil War display, caravan rallies,

(a) Audley End

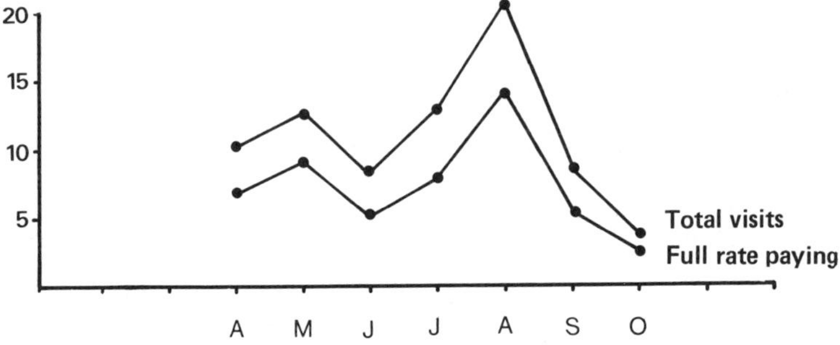

(b) Chedworth

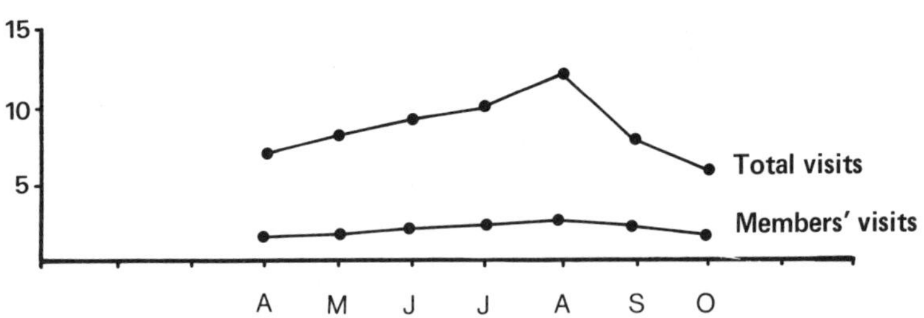

(c) Hidcote Manor Garden

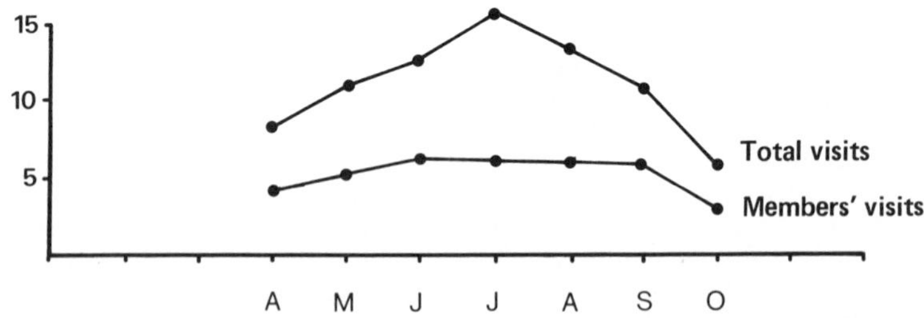

(d) Packwood House

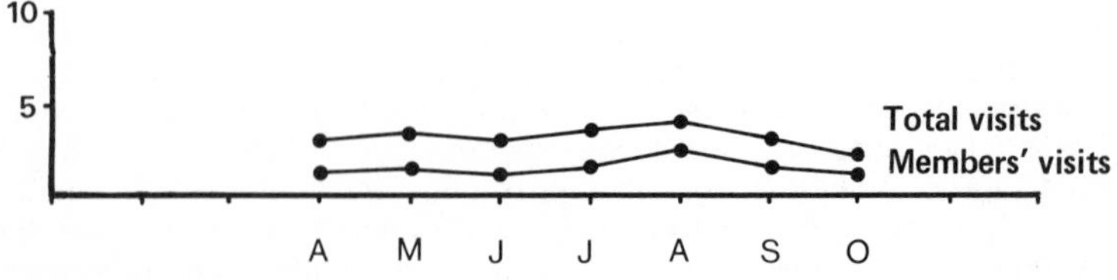

Figure 9.9 Average number of visitors (000) in each month 1978-80

(e) Shugborough

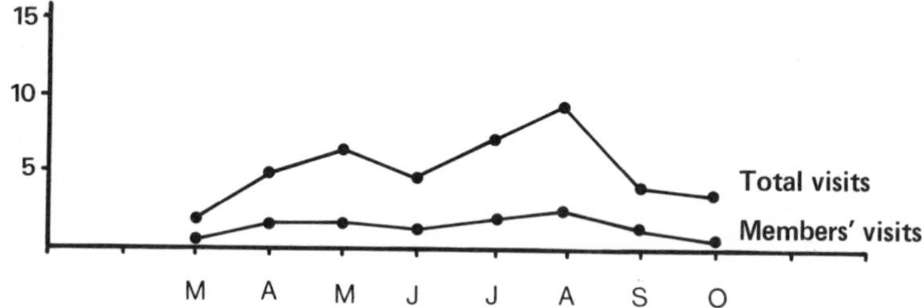

(f) Tatton Hall

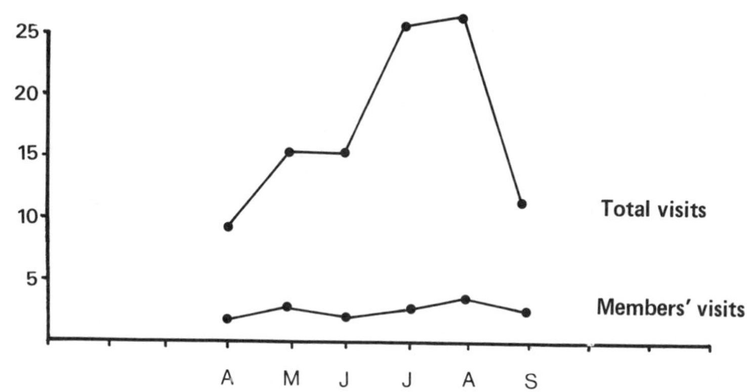

(g) Tatton Gardens

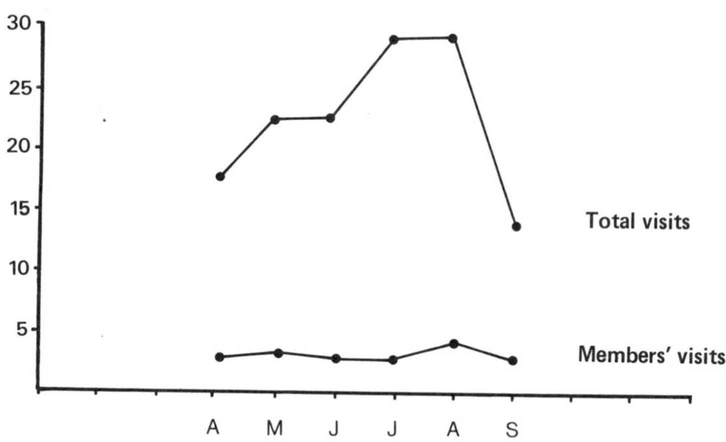

antiques fairs and cross country events. The house is also used to stage a programme of winter concerts as well as for occasional private functions.

All the major public events are usually associated with an increase in advertising. Whilst these do generally produce a marked increase in the number of vehicles entering the park, they appear to have had a far less marked effect on the number of paying visitors to either the house or the gardens. Clearly the success of such outdoor events is heavily dependent on the weather. Between 1978 and 1981 the Tatton Weekend Event attracted between 9,000 and 14,000 people. However, the number of paying visitors to the house and gardens generally dropped off during this event.

The visitor survey carried out in 1978 indicated that very low proportions of visitors were aware of advertisements on local radio (1.4%) or in the northern editions of the national press (5.7%) - both of which had featured heavily in the 1978 advertising campaign. A far higher proportion (23.5%) had seen recent advertisements in the local press. Since this time, therefore, an appreciable proportion of the advertising and promotions budget has been switched from newspaper advertising to television commercials. These are believed to be very effective in producing an increase in the number of visitors and, along with the associated programme of special events, have probably played a part in the growth in the number of visits which has occurred since 1977. Unfortunately, however, it was not possible to obtain data of sufficient detail to pinpoint the precise effects that these initiatives have had on the number of visits.

Summary and conclusions

The results of the statistical analysis discussed in previous chapters were generally confirmed by the detailed examination of factors which have influenced the pattern of visits to the case study sites. The statistical analysis of annual and monthly admissions data and the practical experience of the site managers and administrators indicate that the level and structure of admission charges can have a significant influence on the volume and behaviour of paying visitors. In general, small, regular increases in admission prices appear to have entailed less consumer resistance than infrequent but more substantial increases. In practice, however, trends and variations in the number of paying visitors to individual sites are likely to be modified by a wide range of general and local factors - including variations in the weather, petrol prices and the running costs of private cars.

Available visitor surveys indicate that a disproportionately high number of visitors to the case study sites were drawn from social classes I to III. Social class also appears to have a noticeable effect on the frequency of visits - the trend being for those households in the higher socio-economic groups to make the greatest number of visits. Moreover, even in the case of sites which are relatively close to major urban areas, a very high proportion of visitors travel to the sites by private car.

At several sites the number of visitors attracted at peak periods has placed strains on the site amenities and increased operating/maintenance costs. Whilst there were important variations between individual sites, the peak in the number of paying visitors generally occurred during the July to August period. Subsidiary peaks were associated with the Easter and Spring Bank Holidays.

There is some evidence that the elasticity of demand from casual visitors attracted during peak periods, such as weekends, is somewhat less than those attracted at other times. In the case of National Trust sites, visits from members, which have come to account for an increasing proportion of admissions in recent years, were generally spread more evenly between weekends and weekdays and throughout the season as a whole.

The following chapters extend the analysis by considering in more detail the effects that charging structure may have on patterns of use at countryside recreation sites. Particular attention is focussed on the role that charging policy can play in achieving site management as well as financial objectives and the practical constraints on the adoption of alternative charging structures.

10 The effects of charging structure on patterns of use

Introduction

This chapter examines the issues raised in Chapter 2 on where, when and upon whom to levy charges. It addresses the questions:

(i) In what circumstances should 'all-in' charges be made, rather than separate charges for each major facility?

(ii) To what extent is there scope for differential charges applied to different days, weeks or seasons?

(iii) What would be the effects of such differential charges?

(iv) To what extent is there scope for revised systems of concessions for different types of visitors?

In general, the statistical approaches described in Chapters 6 - 8 cannot provide substantial or unambiguous evidence in answer to these questions. It has, therefore, been necessary to use supplementary sources of information, and especially data derived from the validation case studies described in Chapter 9, to derive tentative conclusions. This lack of data has limited the range of issues on which conclusions can be formulated from this study. However, a number of indications are given of approaches which would allow the analysis outlined in this chapter to be extended and developed.

'All-in' charges versus charges for separate attractions

The issue of where to levy charges involves decisions on whether to charge at entrances, at car parks, for separate attractions within the site or some combination of these. At an early stage in this study, three hypotheses were formulated on the likely influence of the point of charge:

(i) 'Impulse' visitors would be more deterred by 'all-in' admission prices at the entrance, since they are likely to have least information on what this admission price will actually provide.

(ii) Repeat visitors would also be somewhat deterred by 'all-in' admission prices since they might in many cases wish to visit only a selection of available facilities during each visit.

(iii) First-time visitors who set out with the definite intention of making a visit to the site in question are unlikely to be deterred by 'all-in' admission prices since the admission price is only a part of the overall cost of a trip. Moreover, visitors who know the price in advance may regard an explicitly stated 'all-in' price as a positive advantage since they can be sure that it covers most of the necessary on-site expenditure.

Tests on these hypotheses were carried out by comparing information collected by the Mass Observation (UK) Ltd. surveys of National Trust visitors carried out in 1977 and 1978 with the charging structures at the sites surveyed. The facilities included in these surveys were mainly confined to gardens and parks.

Comparison of the results of these surveys with the charging structure adopted (Tables 10.1 and 10.2), suggests that sites which set charges separately for gardens or other facilities tend to be sufficiently large or well known to feature as pre-planned destinations in a high proportion of trips and have a high percentage of repeat visitors. The main exception to this pattern is Dyrham Park which had a below average proportion of visitors who set out with the intention of visiting the site and a slightly below average proportion of repeat visitors. Tables 10.1 and 10.2 also indicate that sites with a range of facilities but 'all-in' charges tend to have a low proportion of repeat visits, except in the cases of Montacute House, Uppark and Little Moreton Hall.

Clearly, firm conclusions cannot be drawn from the relatively small sample of sites included in these tables. However, a number of interesting points do emerge. Firstly, there are some sites, such as Hardwick Hall, Montacute House and Uppark, which did not have a separate charge for admission to the gardens only, yet which did have an above average number of visitors giving the gardens as their main reason for visiting the site and which also had an above average number of repeat visits. Since this survey was carried out, Hardwick Hall has introduced a 'garden only' charge and, while both Montacute House and Uppark gained a high 'value for money' rating from those interviewed in the visitor survey, they also seem to present a <u>prima facie</u> case for considering a separate admission price for the gardens.

For a site with such pull over its market as Montacute House, it may be that it makes commercial sense to set an 'all-in' charge rather than allow a substantial proportion of visitors (potentially about 48% for Montacute House) lower priced admission to only part of the site facilities. Of course, visitor reaction might be even more favourable, repeat visiting even more common and 'impulse' admissions rather larger in number if a 'garden only' charge was made. Certainly, a similar property such as Blickling Hall, with a lower level of visitor satisfaction but a 'gardens only' charge, achieved a much higher percentage of repeat visits than Montacute and a much higher percentage of the visitors interviewed gave the gardens as the main reason for their visit. Again, our validation case study of Tatton Park - where separate charges are made for admission to the park, house, gardens and the Old Hall -indicated that a 70% repeat visit rate was achieved in spite of the 17-18% of the visitors who considered that the price was too high and had some objections to 'paying twice'. Clearly, however, a more detailed and systematic comparison of sites with different charging structures is needed to provide firmer evidence on the effects which charging structure can have upon visitor levels.

Table 10.1

Price structure at selected National Trust sites

Site	Price level	'All-in' charge	Separate charge for gardens only	Separate charge for other facilities	Car park charge
Claydon House	H	√	-	-	X
Oxburgh Hall	H	√	X	-	X
Nostel Priory	H	No	√	√*	X
Lamb House	L	√	X	-	X
Hughenden Manor	H	√	X	-	X
Treasurer's House York	M	√	-	-	-
St. Michael's Mount	H	√	-	-	-
Cornish Engines	M	√	-	-	X
Hardwick Hall	H	No	√	X	√*
Lavenham Guildhall	M	√	-	-	-
Sheffield Park Garden	H	√	-	-	X
Quebec House	M	√	-	-	X
Blickling Hall	H	√	√	-	X
Montacute House	H	√	X	-	X
Uppark	H	√	X	-	X
Penrhyn Castle	H	√	X	-	X
Bembridge Windmill	L	√	-	-	X
Croft Castle	H	√	X	-	X
Trelissick Garden	H	√	-	-	X
Hidcote Manor Garden	H	√	-	-	X
Compton Castle	M	√	-	-	X
Merchant's House Tenby	L	√	-	-	X
Charlecote Park	H	√	√	X	X
Dyrham Park	H	√	√	-	X
Little Moreton Hall	H	√	X	-	X
Upton House	H	√	√	-	X
E. Riddlesden Hall	M	√	X	X	X
Lower Brockhampton	M	√	-	-	X
Peckover House	M	√	X	-	X
Saltram	H	√	√	X	X

Key:

Price level

H £1 or over
M 60p - 90p
L under 60p

Charges for separate facilities

- No facility or not appropriate
X Facility exists but no separate charge made
√ Facility is charged in this way
* Including National Trust members

Source: National Trust

Table 10.2

Visitor patterns at selected National Trust sites

Site	% of visitors setting out with intention to visit site	Gardens as main reason for visit %	% of visitors on repeat visit	Average number of previous visits	Visitors' attitude to admission price V. good value %	Poor value %
Claydon House	89	15	23	2.5	45	1
Oxburgh Hall	91	50	19	3.8	43	1
Nostel Priory	90	26	32	2.6	31	5
Lamb House	61	30	14	1.8	29	4
Hughenden Manor	91	22	14	2.3	28	8
Treasurer's House York	52	12	12	1.7	35	2
St. Michael's Mount	87	20	22	1.7	44	1
Cornish Engines	73	-	17	1.7	34	6
Hardwick Hall	94	32	28	2.4	31	6
Lavenham Guildhall	62	3	25	2.2	38	2
Sheffield Park Garden	93	87	52	3.6	30	8
Quebec House	71	3	7	2.5	35	3
Blickling Hall	97	78	61	4.5	38	1
Montacute House	82	48	31	2.7	45	1
Uppark	93	43	30	2.6	46	0
Penrhyn Castle	79	28	23	1.8	48	3
Bembridge Windmill	63	1	16	1.5	24	6
Croft Castle	81	46	15	2.7	26	3
Trelissick Garden	76	88	43	4.2	28	3
Hidcote Manor Garden	81	94	43	3.4	46	4
Compton Castle	72	15	17	2.1	28	9
Merchant's House Tenby	52	2	18	2.9	50	3
Charlecote Park	96	43	22	2.6	39	1
Dyrham Park	80	46	20	2.9	37	0
Little Moreton Hall	88	84	33	3.5	36	0
Upton House	88	48	23	1.9	44	1
E. Riddlesden Hall	84	28	13	2.0	44	3
Lower Brockhampton	80	13	7	2.6	28	5
Peckover House	91	66	22	1.9	28	0
Saltram	100	42	38	3.5	54	0
(Median)	(84)	(30)	(23)	(2.4)	(37)	(3)

Source: Mass Observation (UK) Ltd. 1978

Comparison of Tables 10.1 and 10.2 also indicates that those properties which had several attractions, but which were least often rated very good value for money - such as Lamb House, Hughendon Manor, Croft Castle and Peckover House - in each case had an 'all-in' charge only and a relatively low proportion of repeat visits. In such cases an 'all-in' charge may represent a sound commercial calculation in that it achieves maximum income from visitors who may be regarded as unlikely to make repeat visits because of the nature or quality of the sites' attractions. This may apply to Lamb House and Hughendon Manor. However, in the case of Croft Castle and Peckover, both of which had a high proportion of visitors who cited the gardens as the main reason for their visit, it is possible that the low levels of satisfaction and low proportion of repeat visits could be partially remedied by the introduction of a 'gardens only' charge.

To provide firmer guidelines on the effects of 'all-in' versus facility charging on demand, it would be necessary to conduct visitor surveys at sites with a much wider range of charging practice, covering private properties, local authority and DoE sites. The National Trust was not primarily seeking information on the effects of charging policy from the Mass Observation survey, which provided much of the data for Table 10.2. However, as the importance of charging policy is gaining increasing recognition, surveys of this type which are carried out in the future should ensure that an adequate range of charging practice is covered by the sites sampled.

In this section, the circumstances in which it may be appropriate to make an 'all-in' charge rather than separate charges for individual facilities have been discussed in terms of their effect on demand. We have not attempted to compare the cost implications of alternative charging systems. The collection costs of alternative charging systems are, of course, an important factor in deciding on the most appropriate charging strategy to follow. However, consideration of these cost implications lie outside the scope of the present study.

Differential charges between peak and off-peak periods

In this section we examine the extent to which there is evidence that demand for visits to individual sites can be smoothed out over time by the adoption of appropriate charging policies. This possibility essentially hinges upon general demand for visits to a site having some degree of price elasticity, so that higher charges set at peak times will deter demand and, conversely, lower charges set at off-peak times will generate increased demand.

The generally low elasticity values identified by the analysis summarised in Chapters 6-8 indicate that the use of admission prices as a means of rationing overall levels of demand at sites might well necessitate large increases above present price levels. Therefore, the aims of site management and of revenue maximisation might go well together for the majority of sites. However, consideration must also be given to the potential equity effects of introducing such price increases. For some individual sites, such as Hidcote Manor Garden, quite high price elasticities have been found and in these cases demand is likely to be much more easily managed by relatively small increases in present admission prices. In practice there is no substitute for each site examining its own price elasticity before making its decision on this point.

If both peak and off-peak demand at individual sites are price inelastic, as overall demand was found to be in Chapters 6-8, then smoothing out visits will require a very substantial differential between the charges. If, on the one hand, peak price elasticity is lower, then it will be even harder to reduce peak demand without introducing wide price differentials, but this would indicate that there was very substantial scope for increasing revenue through a peak pricing policy. If, on the other hand, peak price elasticity is higher than off-peak, demand reduction at peak periods need not entail a large price differential. The fact that the time series analysis described in Chapter 8 yielded strong positive values for monthly dummy variables in July and August, suggests that admission charges during these periods could be raised considerably - but this analysis did not directly indicate elasticity values in those months.

The pattern of visits to the sites selected for the validation case studies followed similar general trends. Visitor numbers were appreciably higher in the summer months than in spring or autumn; July and August tended to be the busiest months; within each month Saturdays and especially Sundays, tended to be the most popular days; Bank Holiday weekends had very much higher visitor numbers than other weekends in the month; and the August Bank Holiday was usually the peak of the year. Nevertheless, there were important variations in the extent and timing of peak periods between sites and these would need to be understood and taken account of in deriving a scale of differential charges.

Since differential pricing for winter and summer seasons was uncommon at the sites included in the present study, it has not been possible to establish whether price elasticities for the winter period are similar to those calculated for the summer period. Of the sites selected for our validation case studies, Chedworth, Packwood and Tatton Park were open throughout the year, but in no case did they levy differential summer/winter charges. Audley End experimented with a longer opening season in 1977 and 1978 but abandoned it in 1979.

During the summer season, the greatest peaking tends to occur at the weekends and Bank Holidays; while this peaking effect is generally greatest in July and August it can place a strain on site capacity in other summer months as well. Since this is the peak demand for the year as a whole, it is the restraint of this demand which is especially important for site management. Administrators for both Hidcote and Shugborough expressed concern about the excess demand experienced at peak times. Furthermore, entries in various handbooks, such as 'Historic Houses, Castles and Gardens' and the National Trust's guide to properties open to the public, emphasise that for some sites peak demand can exceed site capacity. For example, the entry for Sissinghurst Castle Gardens in the National Trust's guide indicates that it is 'liable to serious overcrowding on Sunday'; whilst that for Hardwick Hall notes that it is 'liable to serious overcrowding on Sundays and Bank Holidays'. It is therefore particularly important to determine the extent to which price elasticity at weekends and Bank Holidays conforms to the general patterns discussed earlier.

Experience at two of the sites included in the validation case studies provides some evidence upon this question. At Chedworth, a check was kept on the number of people turning away after reading the scale of charges following the 50% increase in admission charges in the Spring of 1981. While there was an average turning-away of 20-25%, the proportion generally dropped to 11-13% at weekends. This certainly indicates that demand at weekends is rather more inelastic than during the week. Secondly, at Shugborough in 1978 and 1979 a car parking charge was operated only at weekends, entrance to the grounds and museum being otherwise free. The weekend car parking charges were felt by the curator to have helped in evening out the flow of visitors, which had been causing problems at peak periods.

The argument against rationing demand during peak periods at both Shugborough and Hidcote Manor Garden was that it was administratively cumbersome. To this we might add that it seems likely that high differentials would be necessary to have any substantial effect on peak period visits at many sites. However, the benefits, in terms of staff savings, maintenance costs and increased visitor satisfaction, need to be weighed against these problems. Our conclusion is that it does appear to be feasible to ration demand by increasing admission prices at peak times in the case of some sites at least, and it certainly seems likely to be a very profitable approach; however, other policy objectives, especially equity considerations and achieving simplified administration, would not necessarily be served by such a policy. Clearly, site operators and managers need to determine the balance of these issues in the specific context of each site.

To inform decisions on methods of constraining visitor numbers at peak periods and increasing revenue from admissions, there is a major need for systematic analysis of peak period elasticity values separately from the overall elasticity estimates examined in this report. This would entail the study of the pattern of visits at sites which have instituted some form of differential peak pricing - incorporating comparisons before and after introducing such differential charges as well as comparisons with similar sites not using differential peak charges.

Differential charges for different categories of visitor

As noted in Chapter 2, DoE sites almost always allow children and retirement pensioners admission at half price. Practice is more varied at National Trust properties, with pensioners in particular expected to pay the full admission price at many properties. Coach parties are often given substantial reductions, but usually only if they book in advance. In addition, the National Trust operates a membership scheme and the DoE an annual season ticket scheme which provide 'free' entry to all their properties.

Adult/child differentials

It is noticeable that some properties have gradually reduced the differential between child and adult admission rates. Shugborough, for example, charged 20p for adults and 5p for children in 1975 but 60p and 30p in 1981. This trend is more evident at private sector sites. In the validation case studies, site managers were asked what they thought the proper differential between adult and child prices should be. They generally argued that a 50% reduction for children was proper, given the educational benefits from their visits and the fact that they may well be the regular visitors of the future. However, it was observed in some cases that children impose higher costs on sites than adults and, for sites where this is important, there is a case for decreasing or even conceivably reversing the price differential between adults and children.

One rationale for giving concessions to particular groups is that it can help site operators to match demand to the capacity of the site. Confining concessions for parties and large groups to those booking in advance has this effect. It may also be that decreasing the differential between charges for adults and children also has this effect, since visitors to National Trust properties are more likely to take children with them in the months of July and August (28% and 26% respectively) than in June (20%), April/May (18%), September (15%) or October (12%) - (Mass Observation UK 1978). However, the implications for countryside recreation in general, where 61% of trips are made by families with children (Countryside Commission 1981), might be quite different. In making decisions on this issue it would be important to know in more detail the price elasticity of visits by children. Despite the difficulties caused by the fact that children generally make visits jointly with adults, the data does exist for both DoE and National Trust sites which could help to establish whether price elasticity for visits by children is significantly different from the price elasticity for adults.

Equity between social classes and income groups

It is often thought that admission charges act mainly to exclude low income users from facilities and that increases in charges affect this group in particular. Agencies which set a high priority upon equity considerations are therefore sometimes encouraged to forgo or minimise charges in order to promote the welfare of low income groups. This is likely to gain political acceptance when low income groups comprise a significant proportion of the users of a facility and when other objectives are not considered important or can be achieved with a low level of charges. However, visitor surveys carried out at a number of the sites included in the present study and previous research findings have demonstrated that low income households are less likely to make countryside recreation trips than high and middle income households and that households which do not have access to a car make a very low number of trips. Indeed, 85% of all countryside recreation trips are made by car (Countryside Commission 1981). The study of visitors to National Trust properties untertaken by Mass Observation in 1976-77 showed that between 34% and 52% of visitors were in social classes I or II, which comprise 13% of the total adult population (Mass Observation UK 1978). Therefore, a policy of keeping charges for countryside recreation facilities low mainly benefits higher and middle socio-economic groups; it is a very indirect way of improving the welfare of lower income groups.

An alternative method of helping lower income groups as part of an equity objective, is to make concessionary charges to groups defined as deserving special treatment. This has become common practice in the case of retirement pensioners. In the case of facilities operated by some local authority recreation departments concessions have been extended to the unemployed and it is conceivable that households on supplementary benefit could also be included in concessionary schemes. However, the validation difficulties and the stigma attached to them are sufficient to render it unlikely that much headway will be made in introducing more general concessionary price schemes unless a more unified social benefit scheme is introduced, either nationally or in specific local authorities, associated with reliable identification cards for households qualifying for the benefits. Such so-called 'passport' schemes have not yet made much progress at national or local level, although some limited advances have been made in social services (Howes 1976) and some unification of national benefits has been achieved in the Social Security and Housing Benefits Act 1982.

Given the relatively low rates of participation in countryside recreation by households with low incomes and those without access to a car, an agency which puts a high priority on their welfare might consider a policy of explicit provision of new or adapted facilities more likely to cater for these groups. Visitor surveys, or preferably general household surveys, would be needed to establish what types of facilities would be likely to attract lower income groups to new or existing sites. Where finance is a constraint, cross-subsidisation of sites targeted at low income groups by means of higher charges at other sites would promote the equity objective, although it might interfere with the achievement of other objectives.

Concessions through membership and season ticket schemes

The National Trust offers various classes of membership, all of which entitle members to 'free' entry to National Trust properties; the Department of the Environment also operates an annual season ticket scheme, whereby holders gain 'free' entry to its sites. The analysis of such schemes which has been carried out in this study has been confined to an assessment of the effects of site admission charges and National Trust membership fees on visits to particular properties. As reported in Chapter 8, for a minority of sites the ratio of admission prices to membership fees appears to have had a significant positive effect on the proportion of visits accounted for by members. Moreover, it is likely that the overall increase in admission prices has had a very significant effect on the growth of National Trust membership. This hypothesis would best be tested region by region, to establish if regions with rather lower rates of increases in admission prices have shown lower rates of growth in National Trust membership.

What is more significant for site management purposes, however, is that visits by National Trust members tend to display a more even distribution over time than visits by paying visitors and are less markedly peaked. This implies that, if admission prices rise further relative to the National Trust membership fee, then the resulting shift from paying visitors to members' visits is likely to lead to a better distribution of visits over time. However, to the extent that this is simply a reflection of the different trip making characteristics of the average existing National Trust member and the average existing paying visitor, this tendency may diminish as more people become members, since there is no reason for believing that taking up membership in itself changes the days on which trips are made.

Of course, the trend towards members accounting for an increasing proportion of visits to National Trust sites has serious long-term consequences for the revenue directly received by many sites. This has been compounded for some sites by the policy of promoting 'corporate' National Trust membership for organisations and bodies such as schools. The reaction of some sites which are owned by the Trust but managed by other organisations such as local authorities has been to carefully distinguish which parts of the site National Trust members have a right to visit without charge. Charges are then imposed on everything else separately in order to involve National Trust members in at least some expenditure during their visit. This reaction may, however, conflict with the objective of adopting the most appropriate charging structure - for example, in situations where an 'all-in' price would be regarded as sensible. Such a trend obviously directs site managers towards enterprises which can legitimately charge National Trust members, such as shops, catering facilities, craft centres, garden centres, local or natural history museums, exhibitions, etc.

The importance of this external factor in determining the structure of charges at National Trust sites is likely to increase in the future. If it begins to seriously distort the pricing structures which sites would otherwise choose, it may become essential for accounting mechanisms to be found which allocate notional income allowances to properties to compensate for the National Trust members they admit free of charge. These accounting mechanisms are likely to involve reference to the admission prices charged to non-member visitors and this is a further reason for site operators to think carefully about the level and structure of their present charges.

The evidence presented in Chapter 3 suggested that the growth in the numbers of households participating regularly in countryside recreation may well be over, at least for some considerable time to come, and that a larger proportion of visits is being made by a 'hard-core' of enthusiastic households. Given this static market, the National Trust membership scheme appears to have been very effective in achieving the objective of encouraging visits to National Trust properties and more active promotion by other site operators of similar schemes would still seem to be sensible. This would allow them not only to win back some of the 'market share' which the National Trust has taken in recent years but also help to preserve the overall size of the countryside recreation market by tempting some visitors to make more trips than they would otherwise have made.

11 Conclusions on the role of charging policy in the management of countryside recreation facilities

Introduction

The first part of this chapter summarises our main conclusions on the effects of admission prices on visits to DoE and National Trust sites; the effects of charging structure on patterns of use, and the importance of other influences on demand. The second part considers the implications of these findings for the management of analogous countryside recreation facilities, such as country parks, and highlights the importance of setting objectives for charging policy; generating policy options for individual sites; considering the role of charging in the 'marketing mix' and monitoring the effects of charging policy.

Effects of admission prices on visits

The best estimate for price elasticity at DoE sites from the cross-sectional analysis summarised in Chapter 6 was between -0.15 and -0.40. It appeared that price elasticity may well have decreased between 1976 and 1978 and changes in admission prices appeared to have had less influence on changes in the number of paying visitors in 1980. There was also evidence of substantial lagged responses to changes in admission prices in the previous year.

The longitudinal analysis summarised in Chapter 7 confirmed that price elasticities for DoE sites were in the range of -0.20 to -0.30 over the study period. Despite the large percentage increases in admission prices at the more popular DoE sites in the latter part of this period, there was no strong evidence that the price sensitivity of visitors increased more than at sites with lower visitor numbers. The relatively lower price elasticities found by this approach may indicate that the DoE practice of introducing large price increases every two or three years aroused significant short-term consumer resistance.

The time-series analysis described in Chapter 8 gave price elasticity estimates for individual sites which broadly conformed with these results. However, some sites, such as Walmer Castle and Lullingstone Roman Villa, may have had elasticity values even lower than -0.15 and a small number, such as Carisbrook Castle and Osborne House, appear to have had elasticities in excess of -0.40.

These results indicate that there was, in general, substantial scope for raising revenue through price increases at DoE sites during the study period. However, this also means that using admission prices as a tool for restraining visitors at heavily used sites would often necessitate either very large overall price increases or special pricing arrangements for peak periods only.

The best estimate for price elasticity at National Trust sites from the cross-sectional analysis was that it lay between -0.30 and -0.60 for sites with high prices and those with high or medium visitor numbers. However, it appeared that higher priced sites may have had elasticities above -0.60 in 1978. Visits to lower priced sites and those with lower visitor numbers did not, in general, appear to have been significantly influenced by changes in admission prices during this period. There was no indication that price elasticities for National Trust sites had tended to rise over the study period as a whole. The time-series analysis tended to confirm this range of values, although two of the thirteen sites included in the analysis had higher elasticity values in the range -0.80 to -1.05 (Packwood House and Hidcote Manor Garden).

As with DoE sites, it would appear from these results that there was substantial scope for raising revenue through increases in admission prices at National Trust sites during the study period. However, the fact that elasticity values appeared to be significantly higher at National Trust sites indicates that there was likely to be much more scope for restraining visitor numbers at some over-used or vulnerable sites by adjusting their charging policy than was the case for DoE sites.

Effects of charging structure on patterns of use

A number of issues concerning the effects of the structure of admission charges on patterns of use at countryside recreation facilities were examined in Chapter 10. The major points which emerged are summarised here.

Point of charge

There is some evidence that 'all-in' admission charges may not be appropriate for some sites which have a number of important attractions and a high proportion of repeat visitors. Whilst a more detailed and systematic comparison of sites with different charging structures is needed to provide firmer evidence on this aspect, it appears likely that a system incorporating separate charges for separate facilities is likely to prove less of a deterrent to repeat visitors.

Differential peak and off-peak charges

It seems likely from the evidence available that high differentials would be necessary to have a substantial effect on the number of visits during peak periods. Such a policy would, however, be feasible at many sites and could result in savings on maintenance and staff costs, increased protection of the amenities of the site, increased visitor satisfaction and often considerable increases in the income derived from admissions. On the other hand, it would raise conflicts with objectives such as the desire to ensure equity and simplicity of administration.

Differential charges for different classes of visitor

The differential between adult and child admission prices was found to vary markedly between sites, both in the private sector and for National Trust sites. There was some evidence that this was partially related to the higher risk of damage at some properties. It was also suggested that higher child-adult price ratios might be particularly effective in deterring demand at peak periods, when children make up a higher proportion of visitors.

Equity between social classes and income groups

Given the social composition of visitors to the countryside identified by user surveys and by the Countryside Commission's national survey of countryside recreation, it seems likely that a policy of maintaining low charges for countryside recreation facilities will mainly benefit higher and middle socio-economic groups and that it would be a very indirect way of improving the welfare of lower income groups.

Concessions through membership and season ticket schemes

The National Trust's membership scheme appears to have played a significant role in protecting admissions to National Trust properties from the downturn in visitors seen elsewhere since the mid-1970s. It may also have been useful in achieving site management objectives - since National Trust members are more likely to make their visits at off-peak times than non-members. More active promotion of similar schemes by other site operators would seem justified, in order to help them win back some of the 'market share' recently lost to the National Trust and also to preserve the overall size of the market by attracting more regular customers.

The points raised in this section indicate the need to view the design and operation of a charging system as a policy decision which needs to be tailored to the circumstances of different sites and different catchment areas. The general conclusions from the preceding analyses of the overall effects of price increases need to be interpreted in the light of the pricing structures which are currently adopted and the available alternatives. As was highlighted in Chapter 10, there is a need for a much more systematic appraisal of the potential of different charging structures to influence the volume, the timing and the types of visits to countryside recreation facilities. Current practice appears to have greatly neglected these possibilities.

Other influences on demand

The inclusion of weather variables generally increased the level of explanation of visitor trends in the cross-sectional and time-series analyses. Nevertheless, the influence of the weather variables did not come through consistently or markedly in most cases. Not surprisingly, the monthly data used in the time series approach seemed to work better than the annual data in the cross-sectional analysis. There is a strong likelihood therefore, that weekly or weekend weather data would be much more strongly and clearly related to variations in the number of visitors to countryside recreation facilities.

In years when major increases in the real price of petrol occurred (such as 1974-75 and 1978-79) there was some evidence that these played a part in affecting visits to sites. However, in the longer-term there was not a clear and unambiguous relationship between real increases in petrol prices and changes in the number of visits. As admission costs have come to represent a much larger proportion of total trip costs in the 1970's, the importance of petrol prices and car running costs in influencing decisions on recreational trips may indeed have decreased.

As was shown in Chapter 3, the major component of the decline in countryside recreation trips between 1977 and 1980 was in the number of trips made while on holiday away from home. National economic trends and the attractions of cheap holidays abroad (especially when the pound was strong against foreign currencies) have exerted major influences on the number of holidays taken away from home in Britain. Since prospects for future economic growth and for a substantial increase in the proportion of holiday trips made within Britain are not favourable, the catchment areas of many sites may have changed permanently. The origin and timing of countryside trips may also be changing significantly. This will pose new marketing and pricing challenges for site operators in the future.

Pricing and demand for visits to country parks

The results of this study may have implications for a wider range of countryside recreation facilities than the DoE and National Trust facilities included in the analysis. To show how these findings might be interpreted in the context of different but analogous sites, this section provides a brief assessment of the light which the results shed on the nature of demand for visits to facilities which may be provided within country parks.

The most direct statistical evidence on demand for park amenities comes from Chapter 6. There it was shown that changes in admission prices were a statistically significant influence on changes in the number of visitors in every year between 1976 and 1980 for those National Trust sites with extensive parklands. The value of price elasticity for this group of sites ranged from -0.24 (in 1979) to -0.56 (in 1977). These estimates are consistent with, if perhaps a little lower than, the price elasticity values for National Trust sites as a whole reported in Chapter 6.

Some of the properties for which time series analysis was carried out in Chapter 8 are essentially park and garden properties - Hidcote Manor Garden, Sheffield Park Gardens, Stourhead Garden and Tatton Park Gardens fall into this category. While the former two properties had relatively high elasticites, the latter two did not display significant price-visitor relationships. In general, the indirect evidence which the results of this study provides suggests that price elasticity of demand for country parks may be in the same middle range which characterises National Trust properties; but that this might well vary considerably according to the circumstances of individual sites. It seems likely therefore that, as with DoE and National Trust sites, there may be substantial scope for raising revenue from charges at country parks. Again, the scope for control of peak demand by charging may be constrained by the high price differentials which would often be necessary, although this might not apply for all sites.

The equity effects of charging for country parks might be rather different from those encountered in charging for National Trust sites, since it appears that National Trust visitors are more likely to belong to higher social classes than are countryside visitors generally (Mass Observation 1978; Fitton 1979). Furthermore, low income groups are more likely to be deterred by increases in charges. Nevertheless, given the relatively low rate of participation in countryside recreation by low income households and those without access to cars, an agency which puts a high priority on their welfare might rather consider explicit provision of new or adapted facilities more likely to cater for the needs of these groups.

None of these conclusions provide a definitive answer to the questions of whether charging at a country park is justified and, if so, at what level charges should be made. At many countryside sites, the costs of enclosing the site would be much higher than any possible financial benefits could justify. At other sites, the staff and equipment costs of collecting charges might often outweigh the possible benefits. However, this can only be ascertained if the benefits are looked at carefully, site by site, as we have argued above.

For country parks, the context in which we would expect decisions to be made on whether to charge, where to charge and who to charge is set out in Figure 11.1. Three types of site have been identified, each of which caters for different types of recreational experience and involves different levels of costs in order to provide and maintain site amenities.

Type of recreation site	Cost of visitor management	Cost of provision for visitor enjoyment	Charging
Access land	low	low	charging not likely to be necessary
Attraction-natural, something to see	low/high*	medium	charging likely; car parking charges
Attraction-facility, something to do and/ or see	medium/high*	high	admission/ facility charges

* Dependent on visitor patterns, especially peak demand.

Figure 11.1

A framework for charging policy

Costs of visitor management (to maintain the quality of a site) are likely to be low for access land sites and high for those sites where there is 'something to do and/or see' and which experience high levels or concentrations of visitors. Costs of provision for increased visitor enjoyment, on the other hand, are likely to be low for access land, low to medium for the 'something to see' category, and medium to high for the 'something to do' category.

While it is hoped that this provides a useful framework and a guide to site managers, it must be reiterated that the individual circumstances of each site must be considered fully in formulating a charging policy for that particular site. As the Countryside Commission builds up its management information data bank on country parks, it will become possible to test directly the responsiveness of the number and composition of visits to the charging policy adopted - in terms of both the levels of charges and the charging structure.

Setting objectives for charging policy

In the discussions which took place in the course of this study, site operators usually indicated that a relatively narrow range of objectives influenced charging policy in practice. The two major considerations were usually said to be increasing revenue and regulation of visitor numbers at 'vulnerable' sites. Now that charges have become higher in real terms and charging has become a more central issue in recreation management, this narrow focus does not seem satisfactory.

There seems to be a case for arguing that a wider range of objectives needs to be considered. For example, the potential use of charging as a means of throwing light upon visitor preferences has been greatly underestimated. Clearly, distributional objectives might be expected to be important in some cases. In other cases, the social 'spillovers', in cultural and educational terms, from participation in countryside recreation might be regarded as important benefits, with implications for charging policy. While these issues were referred to a number of times in our discussions, and they certainly formed a backcloth to charging decisions, operators did not appear to have taken any explicit steps to modify their general charging policies to incorporate these objectives at specific sites.

It also appears that the logic of the revenue raising and use regulation objectives has not often been followed through. Admission prices in most cases appear to be well below revenue maximising levels; and regulation of demand by differential peak pricing has rarely been attempted. It therefore seems important that site operators - National Trust, DoE and local authorities - should consider explicitly their objectives and their priorities both overall and for each site. This might well result in different priorities being set for different sites in a more systematic manner than has previously been the case.

Generating options for charging policy

The analysis summarised in Chapter 10 suggests that there is an urgent need for site operators to consider their charging structures more carefully and systematically. The major questions which must be answered for each site are:

(i) Is charging through a facility-by-facility charge or through an 'all-in' charge better tailored to maximise revenue and regulate the level of demand?

(ii) Is peak pricing feasible at the site? If so, which method is most likely to meet site management objectives?

(iii) How do the groups qualifying for concessionary schemes and the levels of concessions relate to the site management objectives?

(iv) What is the scope for season ticket sales, joint pricing with adjacent sites, or 'membership' schemes giving 'free' admission to a group of sites?

Some of the issues which need to be considered in providing answers to these questions have been summarised above. However, much more analysis of these charging options needs to be done. Given the often rather arbitrary history of charging structures at specific sites, periodic increases to take account of the rate of inflation is not likely to be sufficient. Infrequent but large price rises across the board are even less likely to allow sites to meet their objectives. More selective approaches are needed, based upon clear objectives set out for each site and upon charging structures, the implications of which have been studied and understood.

The role of charging in the 'marketing mix'

A fundamental fact which this research has attempted to illustrate is that admission price is just one of the factors which site operators have to take account of in deciding their 'marketing mix'. Certainly, it has emerged as an important, and probably increasingly important, factor. However, this report has also highlighted some of the effects which location, weather and property type can have on visitor demand.

From the point of view of site management, the most interesting factors are those which can be controlled by the managers themselves. This category contains a wide range of factors of which the most important are:

(i) admission prices and charging structure,

(ii) opening arrangements,

(iii) quality of facilities provided,

(iv) promotion (general and specific),

(v) special events,

(vi) 'weather proofing' of the site to decrease dependency on good weather,

(vii) 'season proofing' of the site to make the site more interesting for visits (and repeat visits) at all seasons of the year.

This study has concentrated on the first of these factors, admission prices and charging structure, in the belief that it is currently the most critical consideration for site managers wishing to improve achievement of their management objectives. However, as real admission prices increase, the elasticity of demand is also likely to increase (that is, increasing consumer resistance is likely to be encountered). As this occurs, the other elements of the marketing mix within the manager's control will take on extra significance. Already, it is probably the case that some sites are more likely to generate extra revenue by better promotion or specifically tailored events than from general increases in admission prices. Looking at this from a different perspective, sites which increase their charges substantially in the near future may well be able to find simple ways of improving their marketing so as to experience only small net losses of visitors. However, this may eventually become rather harder as real prices climb, so that much more intensive and specialist marketing approaches may be needed to offset price increases, if revenue gains are to be achieved.

Monitoring the effects of charging policy

This book has attempted to provide a much more detailed and reliable picture of the effects of charging policy than has previously been available. It has had to examine critically, and in some cases reject, conventional beliefs about the influence of charges upon visitor numbers, patterns of visits and types of visitor. The conclusions, summarised in this chapter, indicate a much greater scope for utilising charging policy in the pursuit of the objectives of countryside recreation management than has usually been accepted in the past.

It is essential that in future there is not a perpetuation of the misleading and unhelpful myths about charging policy which we have addressed in this study. While charging will certainly not be appropriate at all sites, and only low charges will be justified at others, there may be a great deal to be gained from exploring the scope for extending the role of charges at countryside recreation sites. This can only sensibly be done, however, if the effects of charging policies are closely monitored so that they can be seen to match the circumstances of the sites to which they are applied. This has often not happened in the past.

It is important, therefore, that site operators in future exercise much more selectivity in deciding increases in charges than has been done in the past. Variations between sites in their annual price rises should be seen as the normal and expected practice. Variations between sites in the structure of charges, including differential peak prices at appropriate sites, should also be seen as a rational response to specific local circumstances, the characteristics of sites and the target markets for which particular sites are aiming to cater.

Finally, site operators stand to gain a great deal from the systematic monitoring of new pricing initiatives. This study has indicated that, for many sites, the relatively small deterrent effect of admission prices upon visitor numbers can probably be significantly offset by the introduction of charging structures more carefully tailored to local circumstances. More pricing experiments and pilot studies are needed to gauge the full potential of alternative approaches. These take time and money and require negotiation with the agencies involved. Nevertheless, they offer the major means by which site managers can hope to clarify the potential for achieving their site management objectives, whether it be maximising revenue, regulating demand at over-used sites, responding to visitor preferences or providing for specific client groups. With the growing importance of charging policy, the need for the systematic preparation and monitoring of such initiatives is pressing.

Appendices

Appendix A Estimating demand functions for countryside recreation facilities

Introduction

In this appendix we discuss the sources of data and the statistical approaches used in the study for estimating demand functions. An outline is given of the strengths and weaknesses of each of the approaches used and the likely direction of possible biases in the results is explored.

In Chapter 4, a distinction was drawn between demand for visits to the countryside in general and demand for visits to particular countryside sites. Most households are likely to have smaller price elasticities for countryside trips in general than for visits to specific sites - i.e. an average rise in charges for countryside sites will produce a smaller fall in the total number of trips to the countryside than will an equal rise in the price of one particular site with respect to the fall in its own admissions. This indicates that the demand functions for countryside trips as a whole and for individual sites are likely to be rather different. Ideally, therefore, we should like to estimate these demand functions separately. To do this, however, would require much greater resources of data and time than were available for this study. Moreover, many of the results would be of only peripheral interest to the issues which were central to the present study.

Data sources

The data used in the statistical analyses were derived from the records of the National Trust and the Department of the Environment. In both cases, the data on visitor numbers is a by-product of accounting procedures rather than information assembled for any specific site management purposes.

Level of disaggregation

Cross-sectional data: The basic data used in the cross-sectional analysis comprised information on admission charges and the total number of visitors to National Trust properties and DoE historic houses and ancient monuments in England and Wales for each year during the period from 1968 to 1980. Over this period both data sets displayed sufficient contrasts in the level, extent and frequency of revision of admission charges to allow the price elasticity of demand to be estimated by cross-sectional analysis. The data sets were also sufficiently large for this analysis to be carried out for groups of sites categorised by both the level of admission charges and the number of visits.

The annual data on visits to each National Trust site enabled a distinction to be drawn between the total number of visitors paying an admission charge and the total number of members who were admitted 'free'. Although some of those recorded as paying an admission charge, such as children, would have been admitted at a concessionary rate, the ratio of this reduced rate to the full rate was constant across sites and was subject to similar proportionate increases over time.

The original data set for DoE sites, however, only provided data on the total number of visits to individual sites (rounded to the nearest 100). Consequently this data included not only visitors who were admitted on payment of one of a range of charges, but also substantial and variable numbers of visitors who were admitted free of charge - for example, because they held season tickets or because they were a member of a party making an educational visit. Not surprisingly therefore, preliminary analysis of this aggregated data tended to provide rather poor and variable correlations between changes in admission prices and changes in the number of visits. Consequently, in order to provide more accurate estimates of the price-visitor relationship, it was necessary to extract more disaggregated data from records held by the Department of Environment's Historic Buildings and Ancient Monuments Division. This source enabled a split to be made between visitors paying the full rate for admission, those paying a reduced rate and those admitted free of charge. Unfortunately, however, this source only provided data on sites in England and, due to a change in accounting procedures, only covered the period from 1970 to 1978. For some 36 of the larger sites the data was extended to cover the period of up to 1980 by manually aggregating information from individual monthly returns submitted to the Department by site custodians.

As a result of this data collection exercise we were able to assemble complete annual data on visits and prices for 82 National Trust sites for the period from 1968 to 1980. In the case of DoE sites we had complete data for 115 sites from 1970 to 1978 and complete data up to 1980 for a further 36 of the larger sites.

Time series data: The data used in the time series analysis comprised information on admission charges and visits in each month for a selection of National Trust and DoE sites. Whilst the composition of this 'sample' was to some extent dictated by which sites had adequate records of admissions, as far as possible sites were selected to represent a range of recreational opportunities, locations and admission price levels.

In the case of National Trust sites, data on the total number of visitors admitted in each month was obtained for 13 sites for the period from 1973 to 1980. Assembly of this data set necessitated the extraction and collation of data from records maintained by the Trust's central accounting unit at Melksham, Wiltshire, from the regional offices and, in several instances, from the sites themselves. In some cases monthly data could only be obtained by manually aggregating weekly or daily records. Wherever possible, apparent anomalies in the data obtained were checked against daily and weekly records maintained by site managers. In most instances, these sources provided a breakdown between total paying visitors and free admissions. In some cases it was also possible to split paying visitors into those paying the full rate and those paying a reduced rate.

In the case of DoE sites, monthly data for a total of 32 sites were extracted from the finanacial returns submitted by site managers/custodians to the head office of the Historic Buildings and Ancient Monuments Division in London. For the majority of these sites it was possible to build up a complete picture of visits for the period from 1972 to 1980 disaggregated into full rate, reduced rate and free admissions. Since monthly data was generally only available for the larger, better attended sites, the DoE sample is inevitably biased towards the more popular sites of regional or national significance at the expense of smaller sites of more specialised or localised interest.

For both groups of sites, monthly data was generally only available for the six months from April to September. In the remainder of the year, if the sites were not actually closed to the public, data for months in the winter and spring quarters was usually only available in an aggregated form. Analysis of the time series data was therefore concentrated almost entirely on the summer months during which the vast majority of visits to such sites are made.

For both data sets, particular problems were encountered as a result of variations in the length of accounting periods from month to month and year to year. In particular, reporting requirements of both the DoE and National Trust frequently resulted in a situation in which an accounting month included five rather than four weeks. This clearly makes comparison of visitor figures for individual months within and between years difficult. This comparison is made even more difficult where this feature results in data relating to a Bank Holiday being included in different accounting 'months' in successive years. This problem applied particularly to the periodic movement of the Easter Bank Holiday from April into March. Where it was not possible to adjust the raw data for this anomaly by reference to weekly admissions data, the problem was handled in the course of the analysis by attaching dummy variables to data for months which included five weeks and/or bank holidays.

Types of analysis

Three different methods were employed to estimate the demand functions for these sites:

(i) Cross-sectional analysis of year-on-year changes in admission prices and visits for all sites for which data was available;

(ii) Longitudinal analysis of changes in admission prices and visits between groups of years;

(iii) Time series analysis of year-on-year changes in admission prices and visits in each month for a sample of sites.

The results of these three main types of statistical analysis were validated by more detailed case studies of 6 sites. These validation case studies involved discussion of the results of the statistical analyses with site managers and the collection of further information in order to aid interpretation of the demand functions derived.

Each of the statistical approaches employed provided opportunities to test different sections of the model of recreation trip generation and distribution discussed in Chapter 4. Thus, each of the approaches allowed us to hold some of the factors in the model constant and therefore to explore the effects of changes in the other factors. By doing this, it was possible to build up a composite picture of the actual importance of each of the various factors. The way in which this was achieved is outlined below.

Cross-sectional analysis

For both DoE and National Trust sites it was possible to correlate the change in the number of visitors from year to year with the change in admission prices over the corresponding period, taking account of a range of other variables. Such 'cross-sectional' analysis over a twelve month period has the advantage of highlighting the effect on relative visitor numbers between sites of factors such as weather which experience substantial changes over the same period. Since most of the factors shown in Figure 4.1 which are likely to influence long-term demand and supply only change over much longer time periods, the cross-sectional analysis therefore allows us to identify the separate effects on visitor numbers of changes in admission prices, changes in the weather, and changes in promotion, publicity and the opening or upgrading of site facilities. In practice, however, because of the very large number of sites involved, attention was focussed on the influence of changes in admission prices and weather conditions.

Because this analysis involved correlating changes in the number of visitors over a twelve month period with changes in admission prices and other changes at each site over the corresponding period, we did not need to estimate, nor did we need to know, the overall change in the total number of trips to the countryside between the two years. Instead, our correlation analysis was effectively testing the extent to which changes in the 'market share' of each site were correlated to changes in admission prices (see Appendix B, on estimating changes in market share and absolute visitor numbers). The results of the cross-sectional analysis can therefore be taken to illustrate the effect of changes in admission prices and weather on the distribution of trips between sites for particular years. The results do not tell us the extent to which overall increases in average prices of facilities affect total trips to the countryside. We would expect _a priori_, however, that total trips would be _less_ responsive to price rises than the elasticity values derived from the cross-sectional analysis would indicate. This is because we would anticipate that trips would tend to be re-directed towards cheap or free facilities as average prices for facilities have increased.

Clearly the major constraint on the precision of such estimates is the extent to which it is possible to specify and measure the factors included in Figure 4.1. Since information was lacking on the changes which have occurred in some of these other factors, such as the number and quality of facilities at sites, advertising, special events, etc., the results will inevitably be subject to some error. In particular, if above average increases in admission prices were associated with sites which increased and improved their facilities to an above average degree, or had undertaken especially large promotional or other marketing exercises, then the effect of price increases on admissions will be _under-estimated_.

Longitudinal analysis

The cross-sectional analysis described in the previous section can be developed and refined in a number of different ways. For example, it is possible to take averages of the number of visitors to sites over a number of years and to compare these with a similar average for a later group of years. This change in the average number of visitors over a longer time period can then be compared with changes in admission prices between the two groups of years. For example, in order to gauge the longer-term effects of the large price rise at DoE sites in 1976 we can correlate the change in the average number of visitors between 1973-75 and 1976-77 with the change in average admission prices between these two time periods.

The major advantage of this procedure is that it allows us to increase the number of factors for which we have standardised, and thereby increases the reliability of the results. In particular, by averaging out over a number of years, we can hope to encompass a range of weather conditions which can occur inside each group of years. This means we do not need to include weather as an independent variable in the analysis.

In addition, since not all reactions to a change in admission prices are likely to occur during the year in which it was introduced, grouping data for a number of years allows us to encapsulate the longer-term effects of price changes. Some of the cross-sectional results reported in Chapter 6 indicated that increases in admission prices may produce reductions in visits in the following year. Given the frequency with which increases occurred, it was not possible to build a very sophisticated structure of lagged responses to price changes into our analysis. However, by grouping years in which few price changes occurred and comparing them with other groups of years with different price levels, it is possible to summarise the final effects of price changes, incorporating these lagged reactions.

Finally, by taking groups of years toward the beginning and toward the end of the 1970's, we can also derive values for the price elasticity of demand which are much longer-term and perhaps reflect the fundamental characteristics of recreation behaviour rather than passing trends - which may be extremely volatile, difficult to forsee and consequently of less interest to site managers. There are two qualifications necessary to this, however. Firstly, there may be secular trends which such an analysis would gloss over, and secondly, if there were any significant changes in the facilities available or the promotion undertaken at different sites over the ten year period of the longitudinal analysis, our data will often not pick these up. As with the cross-sectional analysis, if above average increases in facilities or promotion were associated with above average increases in admission prices over the ten year period, then our estimates of price elasticity will tend to be biased downwards.

Time series analysis

For each site for which we were able to obtain sufficient data, it was possible to correlate changes in the number of visitors from year to year with changes in admission prices over the corresponding period. In the time series analysis, we are again investigating the factors which influence a site's share of the total recreational trips made in its region. Because the total number of visitors to the countryside, which forms a site's pool of potential customers, is influenced by many factors unrelated to the site itself, it is unrealistic simply to correlate the number of visitors to a site with its characteristics and its pricing and marketing policies. In carrying out this analysis therefore, account was also taken of a wide range of other factors, including changes in petrol prices, changes in average earnings and weather, which may also be expected to vary over time.

The pronounced seasonality in visitor numbers from month to month, with August being the peak month for most sites, was removed either by incorporating monthly dummies or by regressing change in the number of visitors in a specific month against the change in real or money admission prices in the same month over the period of a year. In this way, the effects of institutional factors such as Bank Holidays and school holidays could be incorporated in the analysis.

Clearly, there are several theoretical and practical difficulties in taking account of all possible factors which may influence a site's market share. In particular, it is difficult conceptually to define precisely the boundaries of the region inside which the site is competing for visitors against other sites, and it is therefore difficult in practice to estimate the total number of countryside recreational trips made within that region. In practice, therefore, we had to estimate trips made each month to a site rather than its market share. For the same reason we were also not able to construct indices of prices or the facilities available or the marketing activity at other competing sites (see Appendix B). What we have therefore undertaken in our time series analysis is an exploration of how one site's visits over time were related to its own pricing levels and a range of other factors which are likely to have influenced regional trip generation, such as variations in weather conditions, income, employment levels, petrol costs, etc. Therefore, data for each site has been used to test the significance of each of these factors in influencing the number of visits.

This approach may have introduced some biases into our estimates of the effect of admission prices on visitor numbers to each site. For example, sites which raised their prices less than the average for similar, competitive sites were likely to have found that they could attract a larger proportion of total visitors than before - but this total may itself have fallen. In such circumstances therefore, our approach is likely to under-estimate the price elasticities of individual sites. The greater is the elasticity of demand for countryside trips and the higher the substitutability of one site for another in the eyes of visitors, then the greater the likelihood of such under-estimation. It would certainly appear that a fruitful area for future study would be the inclusion in a time-series analysis of comparative variables for competing facilities, especially <u>average</u> changes in admission prices, facilities and promotional activities. This would, however, require in-depth analysis of all major competing sites within a region.

A particular problem was presented in taking account of admissions by National Trust members to National Trust properties. Unquestionably, the growth in National Trust membership in the 1970's has influenced the number of paying visitors to National Trust properties. Furthermore, we would expect a systematic upward bias in our estimates of National Trust price elasticity, since many would-be visitors can be expected to have reacted to an increase in the admission price by not paying at the gate (thereby giving us a high elasticity value in our regressions for paying visitors) but instead paying the National Trust membership fee and gaining admittance 'free' at the gates. This acts to offset the downward bias in our elasticity estimates noted in the previous paragraph.

Fortunately, our cross-sectional analysis was immune to this bias, since it estimated the extent to which the sites with the largest price increases over a year had the most unfavourable changes in visitor numbers. Consequently, whether all sites lost or gained as a result of especially large changes in National Trust membership (itself partly caused by the overall level of price increases at all National Trust properties) is not relevant to the cross-sectional approach. However, we have included some analysis of the changing level of National Trust membership and the changing ratio of paying visitors to National Trust members in our time series analysis, as reported in Chapter 8.

Despite the difficulties encountered in undertaking time series analysis, it does have several advantages which allow further insights into particular facets of changes in the patterns of visits. Firstly, it allows us to include the effects of variables which have similar values for all sites - for example, increases in petrol prices and in the retail price index which cannot be incorporated in a cross-sectional analysis. Secondly, it allows us to explore the existence of a time-trend in visits, and differing time-trends for different time periods. Thirdly, it allows a comparison of the elasticity values for individual properties and between different types of properties, whereas in the cross-sectional analysis of the whole data set, different property types were simply allocated different average visitor numbers rather than different price elasticity values. Fourthly, it allows us to investigate much more satisfactorily the influence of variations in weather on visits, since we can use disaggregated weather data rather than the annual data necessitated in the cross-sectional analysis.

On balance then, time series analysis provides a very powerful complement to the cross-sectional analysis. However, the elasticity values derived for particular DoE sites are likely to be minima rather than a precise measure of the average elasticities over the period. In the case of National Trust sites, two offsetting sources of bias occur and it is not possible to say, a priori, which is likely to predominate.

Appendix B Estimating market share and absolute visitor numbers

From Chapter 4 we can summarise the factors which influence the relative share of countryside recreation trips which go to a particular site j as follows:

(1)

$$\frac{V_j}{V} = a_0 \cdot P_j^{a_1} \cdot \bar{P}^{-a_2} \cdot F_j^{a_3} \cdot \bar{F}^{-a_4} \cdot A_j^{a_5} \cdot \bar{A}^{-a_6} \cdot M_j^{a_7} \cdot \bar{M}^{-a_8} \cdot \frac{R_j^{a_9}}{\bar{R}^{a_{10}}} \cdot \frac{S^{a_{11}}}{\bar{S}^{a_{12}}} \cdot \frac{T^{a_{13}}}{\bar{T}^{a_{14}}}$$

where V_j is visits to site j

V is total visits to all sites

P_j is price at site j

$\bar{P}$ is weighted mean price at all sites

F_j is an index of the number and quality of facilities at site j

$\bar{F}$ is the weighted mean value of an index of the number and quality of facilites at all other sites

A_j is an index of the accessibility of j

$\bar{A}$ is the weighted value of the index of accessibility of all other sites

M_j is an index of the effective strength of the marketing strategy at site j

$\bar{M}$ is a weighted mean of the index of the effective strength of the marketing strategy at all other sites

R_j is rainfall at site j

$\bar{R}$ is the weighted mean of rainfall at all other sites

S_j is sunshine at site j

$\bar{S}$ is the weighted mean of sunshine at all other sites

T_j is temperature at site j

$\bar{T}$ is the weighted mean of temperature at all other sites

a_0 - a_{14} are constants

In equation (1) the number of sites considered would depend on a judgement as to the potential catchment area of site j. The weights to be applied to the means of all the other sites for variable P,F,A,M,R,S and T could be assigned a priori, according to how close they are and their 'degree of competitiveness' with j; or they could be estimated by successive runs of the model to achieve improved fit. This formulation assumes a multiplicative relationship which corresponds to the logged function used in the present analysis. An additive relationship could also be shown corresponding to the absolute change function.

If we now compare visits to site j between two different time periods 1 and 2, we get:

(2)

$$\frac{V_j^2}{V_j^1} = \frac{V2}{V1} \cdot \left(\frac{P_j^2}{P_j^1}\right)^{a_1} \cdot \left(\frac{\bar{P}2}{\bar{P}1}\right)^{a_2} \cdot \left(\frac{F_j^2}{F_j^1}\right)^{a_3} \cdot \left(\frac{\bar{F}2}{\bar{F}1}\right)^{a_4} \cdot \left(\frac{A_j^2}{A_j^1}\right)^{a_5} \cdot \left(\frac{M_j^2}{M_j^1}\right)^{a_6} \cdot \left(\frac{\bar{M}_j^2}{\bar{M}_j^1}\right)^{a_7} \cdot \left(\frac{R_j^2}{R_j^1}\right)^{a_8} \cdot$$

$$\left(\frac{\bar{R}2}{\bar{R}1}\right)^{a_9} \cdot \left(\frac{S_j^2}{S_j^1}\right)^{a_{10}} \cdot \left(\frac{\bar{S}2}{\bar{S}1}\right)^{a_{11}} \cdot \left(\frac{T_j^2}{T_j^1}\right)^{a_{12}} \cdot \left(\frac{\bar{T}2}{\bar{T}1}\right)^{a_{13}}$$

where the subscripts to 1 and 2 refer to the year in which the variable is measured.

Cross-sectional analysis

The cross-sectional analysis in the present study took the form:

(3)

$$\frac{V_j^2}{V_j^1} = a_0 \cdot \left(\frac{P_j^2}{P_j^1}\right)^{a_1} \cdot \left(\frac{R_j^2}{R_j^1}\right)^{a_9} \cdot \left(\frac{S_j^2}{S_j^1}\right)^{a_{11}} \cdot \left(\frac{T_j^2}{T_j^1}\right)^{a_{13}} \cdot \text{Type} \cdot \text{Location}$$

where type and location are dummy variables.

This correctly leaves out those variables in equation (2) which can be expected to be common to all sites, namely:

$$\frac{V^2}{V^1}, \frac{\bar{P}^2}{\bar{P}^1}, \frac{\bar{F}^2}{\bar{F}^1}, \frac{\bar{A}^2}{\bar{A}^1}, \frac{\bar{M}^2}{\bar{M}^1}, \frac{\bar{R}^2}{\bar{R}^1}, \frac{\bar{S}^2}{\bar{S}^1}, \frac{\bar{T}^2}{\bar{T}^1}$$

However, it incorrectly leaves out :

$$\frac{F_j^2}{F_j^1}, \frac{A_j^2}{A_j^1}, \frac{M_j^2}{M_j^1}$$

In so far as these may differ significantly from unity ,there may be a bias in the estimation of all the other parameters of the equations. This is, however, partly allowed for through the incorporation of the dummy variables for type and location. Thus, if petrol costs rise significantly, so that

$$\frac{A_j^2}{A_j^1}$$

is less than 1, then the dummy variables for urban and urban-fringe locations should reflect some of this change. Again, if there is any systematic tendency for particular site types to be adding to or improving facilities, this will be reflected in the value of the 'type' dummy variable. If there is no systematic pattern, the equation will be a less efficient predictor but the co-efficient estimates are less prone to bias.

It has been assumed in the paragraph above that the 'all sites' variables are the same for all sites. However, this places great reliance on an adequate weighting system. In practice, the values of these variables for all other relevant sites may differ between sites. In this case, regionalisation of the data sets would substantially improve the estimation procedure. While this discussion shows that the cross-sectional analysis carried out has been far from the ideal estimation procedure, a large proportion of the most important variables have been included.

Time series analysis

The time-series analysis in this study took the form:

(4)

$$\frac{V_j^2}{V_j^1} = a_0 \cdot \left(\frac{P_j^2}{P_j^1}\right)^{a_1} \cdot \left(\frac{R_j^2}{R_j^1}\right)^{a_9} \cdot \left(\frac{S_j^2}{S_j^1}\right)^{a_{11}} \cdot \left(\frac{T_j^2}{T_j^1}\right)^{a_{13}} \cdot \left(\frac{PC^2}{PC^1}\right)^{a_{15}} \cdot \left(\frac{RE^2}{RE^1}\right)^{a_{16}} \cdot \left(\frac{U^2}{U^1}\right)^{a_{17}} \cdot$$

$$\left(\frac{RPI^2}{RPI^1}\right)^{a_{18}} \cdot \text{Type} \cdot \text{Location} \cdot \text{Month}$$

where PC is petrol costs

RE is regional earnings in the region of site j

U is unemployment in the region of site j

RPI is the retail price index

Month is a dummy variable for each month

If we compare this with equation (2), it again incorrectly leaves out:

$$\frac{F_j^2}{F_j^1}, \frac{A_j^2}{A_j^1}, \frac{M_{j,}}{M_j}$$

In so far as these differ significantly from unity in value, there may be a bias in the estimation of all the other parameters in the equation.

More importantly, we cannot confidently leave out from a time series analysis (as we could from a cross-sectional analysis) the 'all sites' variables since they may fluctuate significantly over time. This is especially likely to be true of

$$\frac{V2}{V1}, \quad \frac{\bar{P}2}{\bar{P}1}, \quad \frac{\bar{M}2}{\bar{M}1}$$

and the average weather condition variables.

The inclusion of petrol costs, regional earnings, unemployment and retail price index in equation (4) can be seen as an attempt to provide a proxy for

$$\frac{V2}{V1}$$

It would be preferable, but empirically laborious, to regionalise all the sites and do a two-stage regression for each region in which

$$\frac{V2}{V1}$$

would be estimated in a separate equation from

$$\frac{V_j^2}{V_j^1}$$

The absence of $\bar{P}2/\bar{P}1$ and $\bar{M}2/\bar{M}1$ from equation (4) will mean that sites will have attributed to them lower price elasticities than should in fact be the case at times when their competitor's admission prices are generally rising and/or their marketing campaigns are decreasing in volume or effect. Again, it would be easiest to allow for those factors if the sites were examined on a region by region basis; this would especially help if the regions were chosen to lie wholly within the standard weather regions so that the 'all sites' weather variables could be safely ignored.

On balance, it is believed that the form of equation (4) is likely to lead to underestimates of the price elasticity of demand for individual sites. Significant improvements in the estimates might be achieved by carrying out the analysis for sets of sites within regions.

For National Trust sites, the problems caused by increasing National Trust membership are discussed in the text. This, in fact, provides an offsetting bias in the time series estimates to that discussed above. In Chapters 7 and 8, the results of some separate analyses of the change in the ratio of paying visitors to National Trust members at individual sites are described. The functional forms estimated were, in simplified terms:

(**5**) Absolute change

$$(V_j - M_j)^2 - (V_j - M_j)^1 = a_0 - a_1(P_j^2 - P_j^1) + a_2(F^2 - F^1)$$

where V_j is paying visitors to site j

M_j is members' visits to j

P_j is admission price to j

F is National Trust membership fee

$a_0 - a_2$ are constants

superscripts 1 and 2 denote the year

(**6**) Logged change

$$\left(\frac{V_j^2}{V_j^1}\right) \div \left(\frac{M_j^2}{M_j^1}\right) = a_0 \cdot \left(\frac{P_j^2}{P_j^1}\right)^{a_1} \div \left(\frac{F_j^2}{F_j^1}\right)^{a_2}$$

No appropriate percentage change function could be devised.

Summary

While none of the statistical approaches described in this appendix can be regarded as entirely satisfactory, the range of such approaches available ensures that complementary evidence is available on most of the issues where specific individual approaches are weak.

Appendix C
Relationship between change in the number of visits and change in admission prices

DoE Sites

1969

% Change in Prices	% Change in Number of Paying Visitors 21+	Decrease 20-11	10-1	No Change	1-10	Increase 11-20	21+
No Change	3	8	25	11	43	20	16

1970

Decrease	-	-	-	-	1	-	-
No Change	1	4	3	2	24	16	10
1-10	-	-	-	-	-	-	-
11-30	-	-	1	-	2	1	-
31-50	-	-	-	-	-	-	-
51+	9	8	9	2	18	9	2

1971

Decrease	-	-	-	-	1	-	-
No Change	-	1	19	9	26	38	39

1972

No Change	3	15	17	9	44	20	15

1973

Decrease	-	-	-	-	-	-	-
No Change	-	3	16	3	23	27	24
1-10	-	-	-	-	-	-	-
11-30	-	-	1	1	4	5	2
31-50	-	-	2	1	-	2	-
51+	-	-	3	-	6	2	-

1974

No Change	5	13	45	9	29	20	18

1975

No Change	1	8	31	12	38	21	19

1976

No Change	-	-	1	-	1	-	-
1-10	-	-	-	-	-	-	-
11-30	-	-	-	-	-	-	-
31-50	1	-	7	3	5	-	-
51+	15	22	35	10	13	9	6

1977

No Change	8	14	32	5	26	20	10

1978

Decrease	-	-	1	-	-	-	-
No Change	2	1	2	-	1	1	-
1-10	-	-	-	-	-	-	-
11-30	-	-	8	1	5	1	-
31-50	7	13	30	7	13	8	5
51+	-	-	3	-	-	-	-

1979

Decrease	-	-	-	-	-	-	-
No Change	15	23	38	5	11	9	4
1-10	-	-	-	-	-	-	-
11-30	1	3	1	-	-	-	-
31-50	1	-	-	-	-	-	-
51+	-	-	-	-	-	-	-

National Trust Sites

1969

% Change in Prices	Change in Number of Paying Visitors						
	Decrease 21+	Decrease 20-11	Decrease 10-1	No Change	Increase 1-10	Increase 11-20	Increase 21+
Decrease	-	-	-	-	1	-	-
No Change	6	11	16	3	21	38	25
1-10	-	-	-	-	-	-	-
11-30	-	-	1	-	-	-	-
31-50	-	-	-	-	-	-	-
51+	-	-	-	-	-	-	-

1970

Decrease	-	-	-	-	-	-	-
No Change	1	4	6	1	5	6	5
1-10	-	-	1	-	-	-	-
11-30	1	1	7	2	6	2	5
31-50	2	4	14	2	4	-	-
51+	7	11	5	1	4	3	12

1971

Decrease	-	-	-	-	-	-	-
No Change	7	5	11	4	21	23	35
1-10	-	-	-	-	-	-	-
11-30	-	2	1	1	2	1	-
31-50	-	2	1	-	2	-	-
51+	-	-	-	1	1	-	2

1972

Decrease	-	-	2	-	-	-	1
No Change	11	6	24	6	14	10	15
1-10	-	-	-	-	-	-	-
11-30	3	3	6	-	4	2	1
31-50	-	4	5	-	3	1	1
51+	2	-	1	-	3	-	1

1973

Decrease	-	-	-	-	-	1	-
No Change	6	10	11	6	10	18	13
1-10	-	-	1	-	-	-	-
11-30	1	2	5	1	3	2	5
31-50	1	5	6	2	5	4	-
51+	4	-	3	-	1	1	1

1974

Decrease	-	-	-	-	-	-	-
No Change	5	9	20	-	17	12	14
1-10	-	1	-	-	1	1	-
11-30	-	5	8	2	4	4	6
31-50	3	6	3	2	6	1	-
51+	-	1	1	-	-	-	-

1975

Decrease	-	-	-	-	-	-	-
No Change	4	9	14	6	1	10	19
1-10	-	-	-	-	-	-	-
11-30	2	4	5	3	4	3	4
31-50	2	6	5	2	3	4	2
51+	4	4	1	-	-	-	-

1976

Decrease	-	-	-	-	-	-	-
No Change	-	-	2	1	3	2	1
1-10	-	-	-	-	-	-	-
11-30	-	3	6	2	4	3	2
31-50	6	8	16	2	3	4	12
51+	10	12	21	3	5	3	5

1977

Decrease	-	-	-	-	-	-	-
No Change	3	6	10	3	14	14	12
1-10	-	-	-	-	1	-	-
11-30	3	11	10	1	12	5	14
31-50	-	3	4	-	3	2	2
51+	1	-	-	1	1	-	1

1978

Decrease	-	-	1	-	-	-	1
No Change	2	1	2	-	10	16	20
1-10	-	-	-	-	-	-	-
11-30	1	2	8	-	19	10	11
31-50	2	2	7	-	1	1	6
51+	3	-	-	-	-	-	-

1979

Decrease	-	-	-	-	-	-	1
No Change	2	5	14	4	5	2	5
1-10	-	-	-	-	-	-	-
11-30	9	22	18	-	11	2	1
31-50	3	2	3	-	4	2	2
51+	2	1	-	-	1	-	1

Bibliography

Baxter M J (1979) Measuring the Benefits of Recreational Site Provision, Sports Council/SSRC, London.

Blacksell M (1981) Charging for countryside recreation - a comment, Transactions of the Institute of British Geographers, Vol 6, No. 4.

Bonsey C (1968) 'The rising tide of outdoor recreation' County Councils Gazette, Vol 6.

Bovaird A and Tricker M (1982) The influence of Pricing Policies on Visitor Use of Countryside Recreation Facilities, JURUE, Birmingham.

Bovaird A, Tricker M and Stoakes R (1982) The Role of Charging Policies in the Management of Countryside Recreation Facilities, JURUE, Birmingham.

Butler J (1981) The Economics of Historic Country Houses, Policy Studies Institute, London.

Central Statistical Office (1981) Annual Absract of Statistics, HMSO, London

Central Statistical Office (1981) Social Trends, HMSO, London

Collins M (1977) Long Run Patterns of Countryside Recreation Use, WP3, Countryside Commission, Cheltenhan.

Countryside Commission (1977) Study of Informal Recreation in South East England, WP6, Countryside Commission, Cheltenham.

Countryside Commission (1979) Leisure and the Countryside, CCP 124, Countryside Commission, Cheltenham.

Countryside Commission (1979) Digest of Countryside Recreation Statistics, CCP 86, Countryside Commission, Cheltenham.

Countryside Commission (1980) Rufford Country Park Marketing Study, CCP 129, Countryside Commission, Cheltenham.

Countryside Commission (1980a) Trends in Tourism and Recreation 1968-78, CCP 134, Countryside Commission, Cheltenham.

Countryside Commission (1981) Cragside Marketing Study, Countryside Commission, Cheltenham.

Countryside Commission (1981a) Participants in Informal Countryside Recreation, Countryside Commission, Cheltenham.

CRRAG (1971) Research Priorities, Countryside Commission, London, for Countryside Recreation Research Advisory Group.

CRRAG (1976) Economic Aspects of Countryside Recreation Management, Countryside Commission for Scotland, Perth, for Countryside Recreation Research Advisory Group.

CRRAG (1977) Providing for Countryside Recreation: the role of marketing, Countryside Commission for Scotland, Perth, for Countryside Recreation Research Advisory Group.

CRRAG (1978) Countryside for All? A review of the use people make of the countryside for recreation, Countryside Commission, Cheltenham, for Countryside Recreation Research Advisory Group.

CRRAG (1980) Making the Most of Limited Resources, Countryside Commission, Cheltenham, for Countryside Recreation Research Advisory Group.

Davidson J and Sienkiewicz J (1975) 'Study of informal recreation in South East England', in Searle G A C (ed), Recreational Economics & Analysis, Longman, London.

Elson M J (1979) Countryside Trip Making, Sports Council/SSRC, London.

Elson M J (1979a) The Leisure Use of Green Belts and Urban Fringes, Sports Council/SSRC, London.

English Tourist Board (1978) Planning for Tourism in England, ETB, London.

English Tourist Board (1981) English Heritage Monitor, ETB, London.

Fitton M (1979) 'Countryside recreation: the problems of opportunity', Local Government Studies, Vol 5, No. 4.

Greig P J (1978) Forecasting and Evaluating Demand Response to Recreational Site Characteristics, Unpublished thesis, Oxford Univeristy.

Griffiths G T (1981) Recreation Provision for Whom?, Unpublished dissertation, Cranfield Institute of Technology.

Hendon W S (1982) The Economics of Historic Houses: The Sources of Admission Income, Centre for Urban Studies, University of Akron, Ohio.

Henry I P D (1980) 'Approaches to recreation planning and research in the district authorities of England and Wales' Leisure Studies Quarterly, May 1980.

Hensher D (1977) 'Demand for passenger transport', in Hensher D, (ed.), Urban Transport Economics, Cambridge University Press, Cambridge.

Holman B (1977) 'The price elasticities of demand for ancient monuments', unpublished internal paper, Department of Environment.

Howes J (1976) 'Towards a common assessment scale' Public Finance and Accountancy, Vol 3, No.5, May.

Institute of Recreation Management (1981) The Recreation Management Handbook, Spon, London.

Lees D and Coyne J (1979) 'Can we afford our National Heritage', Lloyds Bank Review, No.131.

McCallum J D and Adams J G L (1980) 'Charging for Countryside recreation: a review with implications for Scotland', Transactions of the Institute of British Geographers, Vol 5, No. 3.

Mass Observation (UK) (1978) National Trust Visitor Surveys, Mass Observation, London.

Miles C W N and Seabrook W (1977) Recreational Land Management, Spon, London.

Miles I C and Smith N (1977) Models of Recreational Traffic in Rural Areas, SR 301, Transport and Road Research Laboratory, Crowthorne, Berkshire.

National Trust (1980) Properties Open in 1980, National Trust, London.

Paul A H (1972) 'Weather and the daily use of outdoor recreation areas in Canada', in Taylor J A (ed) Weather Forecasting for Agriculture and Industry, David and Charles, Newton Abbot.

Price C M (1978) Landscape Economics, Macmillan, London.

Searle G A C (Ed.) (1975) Recreational Economics and Analysis, Longman, London.

Sillitoe K K (1969) Planning for Leisure, HMSO, London.

Snaith R (1975) 'What price heritage: estimating the price elasticity of demand for National Trust properties', in Searle G A C (ed), Recreational Economics and Analysis, Longman, London.

Stoakes R (1976) 'Economic aspects of countryside recreation management', in Proceedings of the 1979 Countryside Recreation Research Advisory Group Conference, Countryside Commission, London.

Stoakes R (1979) Oil Prices and Countryside Recreation Travel, WP20, Countryside Commission, Cheltenham.

Stoakes R (1982) The Effects of the Energy Crisis on Informal Countryside Recreation in England and Wales, Countryside Commission, Cheltenham.

Taylor J A (1979) Recreation, weather and climate, Sports Council/SSRC, London.

Theobald W F (1979) Evaluation of Recreation and Park Programs, John Wiley, New York.

Torkildsen G (1983) Leisure and Recreation Management, Spon, London.

Tourism and Recreation Research Unit (1980) Models of Recreational Travel, TRRU Research Report; No. 33 Edinburgh.

Vickerman R W (1975) Economics of Leisure and Recreation, Macmillan, London.

Vickerman R W (1979) Personal and Family Leisure Expenditure, Sports Council/SSRC, London.

Waterhouse S (1972) Country Parks and the West Midlands, RM17, CURS, University of Birmingham.

White J and Dunn M C (1974) Recreational Use of the Countryside: A Case Study in the West Midlands, RM33, CURS, University of Birmingham.

White J and Dunn M C (1975) Countryside Recreation Planning: Problems and Prospects in the West Midlands, Occasional Paper No.33, CURS, University of Birmingham.

Zetter J (1971) The Evolution of Country Park Policy, Countryside Commission, London.